THE WORLD CLASS PROJECT MANAGER

Also by Robert K. Wysocki:

Effective Project Management
(coauthors: Robert Beck, Jr., and David B. Crane)

Managing Information Across the Enterprise
(coauthor: Robert L. DeMichiell)

Information Systems (coauthor: James Young)

Also by James P. Lewis:

Fundamentals of Project Management
Project Planning, Scheduling and Control
The Project Manager's Desk Reference
How to Build and Manage a Winning Project Team
Mastering Project Management
Team-Based Project Management

THE
WORLD CLASS
PROJECT
MANAGER

A Professional Development Guide

ROBERT K. WYSOCKI

JAMES P. LEWIS

with contributions by DOUG DECARLO

PERSEUS PUBLISHING
Cambridge, Massachusetts

Many of the designations used by manufacturers and sellers to distinguish their products are claimed as trademarks. Where those designations appear in this book and Perseus Publishing was aware of a trademark claim, the designations have been printed in initial capital letters.

A CIP record is available from the Library of Congress.
Copyright © 2001 by Robert K. Wysocki and James P. Lewis

Chapter Seven Copyright © 2001 by Doug DeCarlo

Perseus Publishing is a member of the Perseus Books Group.
Find us on the World Wide Web at http://www.perseuspublishing.com

Perseus Publishing books are available at special discounts for bulk purchases in the U.S. by corporations, institutions, and other organizations. For more information, please contact the Special Markets Department at HarperCollins Publishers, 10 East 53rd Street, New York, NY 10022, or call 1–212–207–7528.

Text design by Tonya Hahn
Set in 11-point Adobe Caslon by Perseus Publishing Services

1 2 3 4 5 6 7 8 9 10–EB–03 02 01 00

First printing, December 2000

Graphics furnished by Lea Ann Lewis and Bill Adams of Adams Graphics, Troutville, Virginia

Art is from Dynamic Graphics, Peoria, Illinois

CONTENTS

TABLES AND FIGURES

Tables

Figures

"What do you want to be when you grow up?" We ask this question frequently and usually get answers like, "Employed" or, worse yet, "I don't know." In today's fast-paced business world these answers aren't acceptable. Too many times we have learned first-hand the horrors of professionals not taking charge of their careers but instead leaving it up to their companies. That is also unacceptable. If you learn one thing from us, you will learn that you own your career and your company owns your job. Don't ever think otherwise. To do so is to risk being passed up in this hectic and ever-changing business environment.

Given that you own your career, the next things you will learn from us are answers to the three most important questions you could ever ask about your career:

1. Who am I?
2. Where do I want to go?
3. How do I get there?

You will find all of the answers you need in the pages of this book.

Since you invested in our book, we can safely assume you want to explore the possibility of becoming a project manager. Congratulations: You have chosen to explore one of the fastest growing and highest demand professions. The help wanted sections of the newspapers and company web sites are filled with opportunities for project managers. Many companies have reported that their business activities have actually been restrained because of their inability to find qualified project managers. That means it will be easy for you to find a job in this profession. For the short term, at least, it looks great but you should also be interested in the long term, and that's where this book will be of most value to you. We are going to help establish a professional development plan for you that will get you started in the right direction and keep you moving along in that direction throughout your entire professional life as a project manager.

Understand right now that this is not an easily reached goal. It will be hard. It will require your persistence and fortitude. It will require creativity. It will require you to take risks. It will require behavioral changes on your part. But acquiring anything worthwhile is going to require effort. You can't expect to be rewarded for simply showing up.

Why Did We Write This Book?

As we said a few paragraphs ago, our profession is enjoying a state of unprecedented growth. The demand for project managers far exceeds the supply and is expected to continue in this fashion for some time to come. Although this sounds great for those of you who want to become project managers, the danger here is that you will be swept up in the feeding frenzy and not be prepared for what awaits you. We want you to be ready when the time comes for you to step up to the plate and hit a home run as a project manager. We have reached a point in the maturing of our profession where executives and senior managers realize they need to put a methodology in place, support it, and—through meaningful training and development of project managers—position it to add value to the enterprise. We know that, and they know that we know that.

This book provides a road map for the growth and development of you—the project manager. It is also a wake-up call for your managers in that it describes an environment they can establish that is conducive to the professional development of project managers and will result in a higher percentage of successful projects. Doesn't this sound like a win-win situation?

What Is This Book About?

This book is really about you. It is our attempt to give you a reference and a guide to help you grow to become the best project manager you can be. It is a book you will want to personalize with your own vision, mission, tactical action plans, skill assessment, and professional development plan. It is a diary for you to fill with all of your hopes, dreams, and aspirations as you begin a lifelong journey toward being a best-in-the-class project manager. Whatever your final goal as a project manager might be, we have crafted a book to help you assess who you are, determine where you want to go, and then help you figure out how to get there.

What Is This Book Not About?

This book is not about project management tools and techniques. There are dozens of excellent books—several of them by us—that will help you learn about project management. Instead, in this book we focus on you, the project manager. What does your environment look like? How can the organization help or hinder your growth and professional development? How can you find and take advantage of the development opportunities your job affords you? What does it take to be a successful project manager? How can you assess your skills in relation to those needed to be an effective project manager? How can you put a plan together to realize your goals and the strategies for acquiring the needed skills?

Who Should Read This Book?

If you have decided to become a better project manager or, perhaps, for the first time, pursue a career in project management, this book is for you. For some of you, project management will be your prime activity. For others, it will only be an occasional activity. You already may be working as a design engineer, lab technician, book production manager, software consultant, or as any other professional and have come to the conclusion that to improve your primary avocation, you need to add project management skills to your tool kit. This book will do that for you. In any case, regardless of your major professional activities, you will want to improve your abilities as a project manager. Whether occasional or full-time, there are several levels of attainment. If you are a "wanna-be" project manager, we will give you a strategy for getting started as a team leader and then progressing a step at a time from team leader, to project manager, to senior project manager, and finally to program manager and even beyond. Depending on your goal, you may want to stop along the way and spend more time in a particular position or spend all of your time in that position. It's your choice, and we will help you regardless of your final destination.

Because this book is also a wake-up call to senior management, they will find value in what we have to say. In Chapter Nine we share several observations on how the organization can help or hinder the professional development of its project managers. These observations become the basis upon which senior management can take action.

How to Use This Book

There is only one way to use this book and that is to start at the first page and read through to the last page. Along the way there are exercises for you to complete, and since many of them build on previous ones, you will need to read this book in the sequence it is presented.

DEDICATION

With the permission of his family and our publisher we are dedicating this book to Ned Herrmann. Ned passed away in December 1999, during the time when we were working on this book. It was our distinct pleasure to have known him and to have worked with him. He never really knew how influential he has been on the work we have been doing with his Herrmann Brain Dominance Instrument (HBDI)—some of which is reported here. For those not familiar with the HBDI, it is a 120-question instrument that measures the four thinking styles of an individual. We knew from our brief encounter with Ned that he truly loved his work and that he made a difference. He would stop and talk about his HBDI at the slightest provocation, and we appreciated him for that openness. We will always carry his memory with us as, with the grace of God, we are able to continue our work with his family to develop further applications of the HBDI in the project management profession.

AUTHOR'S NOTE

William E. "Ned" Herrmann

Ned Herrmann was at ease equally in the classroom, the office, the artist's studio, the research laboratory, and the boardroom. In each of these situations he aspired to be a "living example" of the whole-brain concepts he developed. For the last fifteen years of his life he dedicated himself to applying brain dominance theory to teaching, learning, increasing self-understanding, and enhancing creative thinking capabilities on both an individual and a corporate level. Ned's contribution to the universal application of brain dominance brought him worldwide recognition. In 1992, he received the Distinguished Contribution to Human Resource Development Award from ASTD—an honor that symbolizes the significance of Ned's work. He keynoted world conferences on Creativity; Gifted and Talented Children; Instructional Systems Design, Training and Development; Creative Management; and Cerebral Dominance—just in the last few years. In 1993, he was elected president of the American Creativity Association. Ned was inducted into the HRD Hall of Fame in February 1995 at the Training '95 Conference in Atlanta. He received an honorary doctorate of science from the University of Alaska at Fairbanks in May 1995, and an honorary doctorate of humane letters from Franklin University in December 1995. In April 1997, The Innovation Network presented Ned with a lifetime achievement award for his contribution to creativity and innovation.

Though known today as a master of human resource development, in college Ned studied the sciences and performing arts. He majored in both physics and music. This dual interest in both the arts and sciences seemed to pull him in two different directions but continued to intrigue him throughout his long career with General Electric. With this background, Ned was well prepared for what eventually would become his life's work: to integrate the scientific study of the brain with the study of creative human development, in his search for the nature and sources of creativity.

Ned became manager of management education for GE in 1970. With his primary responsibility of overseeing training program design, the issues of how to maintain or increase an individual's productivity, motivation, and creativity were serious concerns. A prolific painter and sculptor himself, personal experience was a valuable resource. Ned's participation in an art association panel on creativity first opened his eyes to the burgeoning research on brain function, particularly with regard to the left and right hemispheres of the cerebral cortex. He integrated his own concepts with left brain–right brain and Triune brain theories into a new "brain dominance technology," which produced immediate and dramatic advances in an individual's self-understanding, productivity, motivation, and creativity.

In 1978, Ned created the Herrmann Participant Survey Form to profile workshop participants' thinking styles and learning preferences in accordance with brain dominance theory. Sponsored by GE, he developed and validated the HBDI; the Whole Brain Model; and designed the Applied Creative Thinking (ACT) Workshop, which is internationally recognized as a leading workshop on creative thinking.

Ned has been featured in *Business Week, New Age Journal, Discover, USA Today, Training*, and *Reader's Digest*. These are just a few of the many national as well as international publications that have acknowledged his work. He was named Brain Trainer of the Year in 1989 by ASTD, and is included in the *Executive Excellence* magazine's listing of one hundred personalities with unique perspectives on management and leadership.

Ned's first, successful book, *The Creative Brain*, available in paperback, allows laymen and professionals to benefit from his knowledge of thinking and learning styles, brain function, creativity, and training.

His second book *What Will I Be When I Grow Up?*, an illustrated guide for all ages explaining how awareness of mental preferences can improve important life decisions, will be published soon. Ned's third book, *The Whole Brain Business Book*, published by McGraw-Hill, was released for distribution in March 1996 and is already into its second printing. His fourth book, *The 360° Entrepreneur*, is in progress.

Ned is survived by his wife, Margy, and his three daughters, Ann, Pat and Laura, who are actively involved in continuing the legacy that he has left.

chapter 1

The Changing Environment of the Project Manager

Introduction

We live in economic times that have no parallel in history. Technology has created opportunities for businesses that far outnumber their capacity to assimilate. Regardless of the innovative uses one company finds for the application of a technology to a given problem, some other company will find a better one tomorrow. There can be no resting on your laurels in today's business world. To do so is to be passed by, by companies that are ever-vigilant and ever-watching—and don't assume these are established companies. They are not. In fact, many of them are brand-new and are basing their future on that new idea, that new use of technology to meet an established need in the market.

The business world has changed and continues to change at an increasing rate, and with it your world as a project manager is changing as well. What are some of those changes?

The Demand for Project Managers Exceeds the Supply

Tom Peters, writing in the May 1999 issue of *Fast Company* ("The WOW Project," pgs. 116–125), says: "All white-collar work is project work." And "Distinguished project work is the future of work. . . ." If you accept his premise, two conclusions follow immediately. First, everyone must acquire project management skills, and every job will require project management skills. Easily said, but the reality of it is quite different. Second, everyone must become some type of project manager. Wow (not to be confused with the WOW Project)! That makes this book all the more important to you. As you will find out, there are several varieties of project managers. Which one you want to become and how you will get there is very important to your professional future. Read on!

> **"All white-collar work is project work.**
>
> **"Distinguished project work is the future of work . . . "**

Every day the following scenario repeats itself in every business on the planet. You are met by your manager in the coffee room outside your office. She says, "Dale, Pat gave notice to me this morning. He will be leaving the company at the end of the month. You know that Pat has been managing the Alpha Project. The success of this project is critical to our maintaining a competitive pricing strategy in the market. We'll need a new project manager, and I will not be able to fill Pat's position from the outside. I looked at our current staffing schedule, and you are the best choice to replace Pat on the Alpha Project. Congratulations." Sounds good. Dale gets a chance to be a hero. But don't be too hasty. The congratulations may be hollow and are definitely premature. Dale knows little to nothing about project management, having been on a few small projects as a team leader but never as a project manager on a critical project such as the Alpha Project. But let the record show that Dale is now counted among an army of project managers, many of whom have little formal training or experience in project management. Time will tell whether she was in the wrong place at the wrong time. She may be the best choice, but that doesn't make her a good choice. This is all symptomatic of a growing shortage

The business world continues to change and with it your job as project manager.

of qualified project managers. Many companies are trapped: Despite their best efforts to get qualified project managers, there just aren't enough to go around. The growth in their numbers isn't keeping pace with the growth in demand. The result is that less than qualified people are being placed in project management responsibilities. The situation is further aggravated because there isn't time for them to get the training they need—there is too much work to be done, and most projects are behind schedule.

Obviously there is plenty of room for you in this growing profession, so don't spend too much time worrying about getting a job as a project manager. Instead, spend your time planning and considering ways to get there without killing your career. Helping you do that in a sensible and productive manner is the reason we wrote this book.

The Changing Organizational Landscape

It's no secret to anyone that the business world has changed and continues to change at breakneck speed. No sooner do we get used to a certain technology or way of doing business than things change and we are back to the starting blocks once again. Those changes include mergers, acquisitions, major redirection of a company, and the dreaded reorganization, which tends to bring productivity and progress to a halt while all of the chairs are being rearranged.

We have a client that has been struggling to establish a project support office since November 1999, and we just learned (as of March 2000) that they have decided to split into four companies. Guess what—all the balls are in the air, and no one is sure what to do next. Pity the poor project support office director. At this writing he has gone into a holding pattern to await the settling of the dust before he can move forward with any reasonable assurance that what he does is in fact progress. You are probably aware of similar circumstances in several other companies.

Coupled with this ever-changing scene is the constant pressure on us from our managers to work faster, harder, and smarter, and often with fewer resources. Customers now demand, and in most cases will get, instant gratification. If you don't do it, they will find someone who will. "Change or die" is a message that jumps off the pages of John Naisbett's book *Megatrends 2000*. We would all do well to take his admonitions to heart and put them into practice. In the face of this environment the good news is that the changes bode well for those of you who have made a commitment and are serious about becoming the very best project management professionals you can be. The bad news is that the environment is unfriendly and cruel at times. It is not for the faint of heart. We choose to mention this early, not to scare you away but rather to help you face the realities of being a project manager. We will have a lot more to say about this in Chapter Seven.

Right-sizing, Downsizing, Capsizing

In their efforts to keep their stockholders happy, organizations have had to reduce costs and at the same time satisfy an insatiable customer appetite for immediate gratification. Since payroll is usually the largest single item in the company's budget, that is the first place senior managers will look to reduce costs. They generally adopt one or both of two approaches: replace the higher salaried, more skilled and experienced worker with the lower salaried, young and inexperienced worker and/or reduce the size of the workforce through normal attrition, buyout packages, and layoffs or some combination of the three. The loss of the higher salaried people means that the organization may have lost the wisdom and best practices of its experienced staff. In some cases they lose the only person who has a skill that is still needed but not possessed by any of the remaining staff. In any case, the strain on those who remain is greater because the workload does not decrease proportionately with the size of the workforce.

As an aside, Bob Wysocki was recently at a client site conducting a project management training session. On the morning of the second day the director of training asked for a few minutes of class time before the day began. She announced to the group that the training department was being disbanded effective immediately and that all of its staff would be reassigned or terminated. She left immediately after making the announcement. Later that day Bob was having lunch with her and a few others from the training department. Some were being reassigned in the company, and the others were being terminated. Those who were being reassigned were eagerly waiting to find out where their new assignment would be. Those who were being terminated had been offered generous separation packages and were excited about the new challenges that awaited them. The topic of discussion was whether it was better to be terminated or better to be kept on. After both sides expressed their thoughts, the conclusion of the group was unanimous: It was better to be terminated. Are you surprised at their conclusion? Let's look at their rationale. The major reason for their conclusion was that those who remained would have to absorb the work of those who had been terminated. In an already resource-strained environment, it would be difficult, if not impossible, to maintain a sane and rational work life in the face of added responsibilities to an already overburdened and underbudgeted position. To be successful in such an environment would be difficult at best.

In many organizations where these cost-reduction strategies have been implemented, the results are often less than satisfying. Costs might be reduced, but so might revenues and so a second round of cost reductions is needed. The result is the beginning of a vicious downward spiral. Capsizing is the final destiny of many of these strategies. The better alternative might have been to balance cost-reduction initiatives with revenue-enhancement initiatives. They could have put some focus on the revenue side of the ledger and invested in the workforce to improve productivity and revenues and hence favorably impact the bottom line. Remember that effective project management practices can favorably impact productivity and reduce costs as well. There are many examples of how project management can reduce time to market. The interested reader can consult a recent book by Eliyahu M. Goldratt, *Critical Chain: A Business Novel* (The North River Press, © 1997). Although it is beyond the scope of this book, there are any number of time-compression gains that can be realized from the use of template work breakdown structures for those who are familiar with that approach. Don't worry if these two concepts are beyond your level of understanding. The significant thing for you to remember is that project management offers a number of tools and techniques that can favorably impact time to market and productivity. The interested reader can consult any number of books on project planning and control for more details.

Customer Focus

Someone once said that if you don't support the customer directly, you'd better support someone who does. We suspect that for those

who don't do either, a fair question might be: "Then why are you here?" We no longer get paid for simply showing up. Much is demanded of us, and we must be ready to deliver. Time to market has become a critical success factor (CSF), and it is through an effective team of project managers that this CSF depends.

As a project manager in this customer-focused world there will be many opportunities for you to grow and excel. All you have to do is recognize those opportunities when they arise and have a game plan in place for taking advantage of them. That is the topic of discussion in Chapter Six, where we talk about the WOW Project. Because of the fast pace of change and the organizational restructuring to a customer-focus, many companies are in uncharted waters. Anyone with a convincing proposal for doing something differently or faster or more effectively will have an opportunity to contribute and add value. The project manager is in an excellent position to do just that. But you have to be prepared and ready to act.

The Migration from Function to Process

As we have been discussing, successful organizations are customer-focused. To become customer-focused means that the organization had to go through a migration from a function orientation to a process orientation. That is no easy task. The detailed steps to do this are documented in books on business reengineering and are not repeated here.

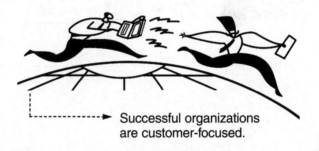

Successful organizations are customer-focused.

Suffice it to say that a successful migration requires retooling the workforce so that it is multidisciplinary, and that is no easy task, either. But the advantages to the aspiring project manager are substantial. Working within a process structure offers a rich source of learning opportunities in a variety of business disciplines. For example, an order- entry to order-fulfillment process will include a variety of business operations such as order taking, order tracking, invoicing, credit checking, purchasing, distribution, collections, shipping, inventory control, return materials control, and others. Your professional development plan may include stints in those processes that will provide those broadening learning opportunities. Besides adding breadth to your skill profile, you can add depth. No matter what discipline you now practice, the opportunity to learn more about project management will deepen your skills in that area. Project management is a robust discipline. Learning it in one area of specialization allows you to transfer it to others, thus increasing your value in the process-oriented organization. If you pick the processes right, you can reap big development rewards. We will have more to say on this topic in Chapter Six, where we discuss the opportunities and obstacles to project manager career growth within the context of various organizational structures. Also, in Chapter Six we'll take a look at the realities of these structures because they can be unfriendly and a challenge to even the most able among us.

The Alignment of the Workforce

It is incumbent upon the organization to keep the skill profile of its project managers in line with the demand for skills by the various business units and project teams. The strategy for accomplishing this will vary depending upon the type of organizational structure in place. For you, the significance of this lies in your ability

> **Some organizational structures make it very difficult for you to deepen and broaden your project management skills.**

to identify and take advantage of the opportunities for professional development that are inherent in these organizations. Be clear, however, that not everything is on your side. Some organizational structures make it very difficult for you to deepen and broaden your project management skill profile. See Chapter Six for further discussion of the impact of organizational structures on the professional development of the project manager. In Chapter Seven we put all of this in focus and talk more about the environment in which you will be working and the challenges that that environment places before you.

The Project-based Enterprise of the Future

All of the factors discussed above are contributing to the unprecedented growth of project management as a profession. As of this writing the demand for qualified project managers far exceeds the supply, and there is no end in sight. Our opportunities for growth in the profession are limited only by our own creativity and initiative. We can grow up to be whatever level of project manager we want to be.

The career path model that we introduce in Chapter Two is rich with alternatives for you to consider. Project management may be an end state for your career, or it may be a transition point for you to move on to internal consulting or people management as further professional growth.

The Changing Individual Landscape

Coupled with the rapid changes taking place in the business world are equally significant changes taking place in the workforce and how it values jobs in relation to careers. Somewhat in reaction to the employer's lack of loyalty to the worker is the worker's lack of commitment and loyalty to its employer. Mergers, acquisitions, and stockholder loyalty have led to widespread downsizing and layoffs and have contributed to the worker feeling more like a commodity than an asset. No wonder we have evolved to a position where the decision to change jobs is based more on immediate gratification from 10 percent to 20 percent salary increases and signing bonuses than on any professional advancement that may result from the job change. While we understand the temptation of job-hopping for dollars, which is a short-term perk, we are more concerned about the long term impact on your professional development.

Because of a national unemployment rate hovering around 4 percent—the lowest in nearly thirty years—enlightened employers are increasing their efforts on retention more so than on recruitment. We see several programs emerging, such as

- training and development programs that align with the goals of employees;
- needs and skill assessment that focus on development of the worker;
- flextime, telecommuting and other programs aimed at improving the work environment.

The alternative to these retention efforts is to continue a recruiting and hiring program. Because of the low unemployment rate, the pool of candidates consists largely of the inexperienced, the unskilled, welfare-to-work people, recovering addicts, and the senior population. Although these populations deserve every chance to be productive members of society, they are not qualified to meet the demand for project managers.

Stepping Outside of the Box

"The job" is an artifact of the industrial revolution. Current thinking suggests that the job is disappearing, to be replaced by "doing what work needs to be done." That means the boundaries created by "that's not part of my job description" are disappearing, too. So what? If you

> **. . . to get ahead, you have to step outside the box.**

stop to think about it for a moment, you will realize that to get ahead, you have to step outside the box. This dejobbing trend is creating an environment that will be supportive of stepping outside the box. For those who have some initiative and are willing to take the risk, there are opportunities for growth.

To be that great project manager that you want to be means that you will have to take some initiative. That means you will have to step outside the box and do some things that are not on your job description. We are going to show you how to seek out and find those opportunities that exist in your organization and that will propel you forward in your career. Tom Peters, writing in *Fast Company* in May 1999, talks about WOW projects—those that offer you an opportunity to learn something new that is needed to advance your career as a project manager. While Peters focuses on project manager roles in choosing WOW projects, we are going to focus at a more detailed level by looking inside projects for those career growth opportunities. When you find one, seize it! We'll show you how it's done.

Multiple Skills

With greater frequency, projects are becoming cross-functional and process related. In addition to personal, interpersonal, general management, and of course project management skills, these projects all require a set of skills that include several business functions. For example, consider the business functions that are present in a process that begins with order entry and ends with order fulfillment. You would expect to see sales, credit verification, order entry, scheduling, billing, accounts receivable, inventory control, packaging, shipping, return materials processing, and perhaps others. As project manager for projects involving this process you would be expected to at least understand the terminology and have a working knowledge of the business processes involved.

The Value-added Worker

If you wish to remain employed by the contemporary organization, you will have to demonstrate to your manager that you have added value to your organization. To be that value-added worker you will need to look creatively at the opportunities available to you and take some initiative to make a difference. This will be risky, but that's the name of the game you have chosen to play. Remember, you don't get paid for simply showing up! We are going to share a key strategy with you in Chapter Eight. The strategy is proactive and will help you iden-

Demonstrate your value to the organization

---

tify needed professional development; how to find it in your organization; and how to take advantage of it.

Taking Charge of Your Career

Most important of all we ask you to remember the one simple fact in becoming a successful professional: Your company owns your job, but you own your career; don't ever default that ownership to your company. If you are fortunate, you work in an environment that is supportive of your professional goals. Such organizations will be of tremendous value to you personally, and you will want to seek out those opportunities that are provided to you. If you don't work in such an environment, it simply

> **Your company owns your job, but you own your career; don't ever default that - ownership to your company.**

means you are going to have to be more self-reliant. We'll discuss this in more detail in Chapter Eight.

Summary

Now you have the big picture. We have discussed the changing business environment and how it impacts on your life as a project manager. These changes in the business environment have brought with them changes in the individual's environment. The individual is now placed in a situation where their professional growth and development is in their hands. No longer can professionals depend on the company to take care of them. With this newfound independence and need for self-sufficiency comes the need for a survival strategy and game plan to thrive and grow in today's business world.

In this chapter we have tried to set the stage for the rest of the book. You have a basic understanding of how project management fits in with the changing business scene. Let us move forward and develop the details and give you a plan for becoming a successful project manager.

chapter 2

So They Want You to Be a Project Manager

Introduction

Not everybody is destined to be a project manager. And for those who want to be one, there are several variations of project manager to consider. As we will show you in Chapter Four, it will take a very special set of skills regardless of the type of project manager you wish to be. Furthermore, the type of project you want to manage will require a set of skills particular to that type of project. The good news is that these skills can be acquired with patience and initiative on your part. We'll describe exactly what those skills are, give you a tool to measure where you stand with respect to those skills, and then in later chapters help you develop a plan to acquire them.

Project management is the "in" thing at the present time. More and more people are becoming project managers. Certificates and degree programs are being offered by colleges and universities throughout the country. Conferences are cropping up at an unprecedented rate. You would think we had discovered the holy grail of management.

Yet people have been managing projects for thousands of years. The first project managers built the Pyramids; Stonehenge; the Maya, Aztec, and Inca temples; the Roman roads; the Great Wall of China; and many other marvels.

Not every-one is destined to be a project manager.

So the discipline is very old. Why all the fuss, then? Perhaps because we have finally realized how useful the skills of project management can be. Perhaps it is because organizations are trying to run "lean and mean," by downsizing, right-sizing, or whatever. Perhaps it is because our world is so turbulent today, and we are trying to bring order out of chaos. No doubt all of these are factors.

In any case, one indicator of the growth in project management is the growth of the professional association the Project Management Institute (PMI). In 1970 they had approximately 5,000 members, after twenty years of existence. In April 2000, the figure had reached 57,000, and approximately 1,300 new members are being added every month. Likewise, professional associations are being formed in Russia, Europe, Australia, and elsewhere. (For information on how to contact these associations, see Appendix A.)

Another indicator is the growing number of master's degree in project management programs and the large enrollments that they are experiencing. George Washington University started a program in September 1996, and by the following September their enrollment had already reached 150. As of January 2000 *Peterson's Annual Guide* listed over twenty institutions offering advanced degrees in project management. For an up-to-date listing, we refer you to their Web site: http://www.petersons.com/graduate/select.

Finally, a significant indicator of how important project management is may be given by the number of project scheduling software programs (of which there are more than one hundred PC products alone) that have been sold. Microsoft, with over 80 percent market share, has sold over 1 million copies of Microsoft Project. This means that at least a million individuals have felt a need to try to schedule projects. No doubt there are many more who manage projects without benefit of any scheduling software. In seminars taught by Jim Lewis, only about one-third of participants are using software regularly. If this ratio holds true nationwide, then perhaps 3 million people are actually managing projects without using scheduling software. Of course, this is totally speculative. All we can say is that there is definitely a lot of interest in the profession.

Is It All Just a Passing Fad?

For the United States, it is reasonable to ask if this interest in project management is just a passing fad. After all, we have tried all kinds of "quick fixes" since 1980, when quality circles became all the rage. You would be hard-pressed to find many quality circles in the United States today. Will project managers also become extinct when the candy coating wears off the pill? If so, should you invest in a career that might not take you anywhere?

We have talked with a number of experts in the field (see our interviews in Chapter Three), and most of them believe that it is not just a fad. The reason is that project management is a specialized discipline, providing skills needed to manage a project successfully. Since it is

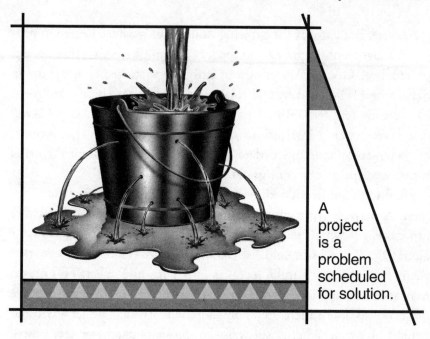

A
project
is a
problem
scheduled
for solution.

hard to imagine a world without projects, it seems likely that the profession will endure.

A better question might be, then, "Do I want to be a dedicated, full-time project manager or an occasional project manager?" We will define the occasional and the dedicated project manager in this chapter and help you answer this question in Chapter Four. For now, we will discuss what project management is all about—for the occasional and for the full-time, dedicated project manager.

What Is a Project?

Before you know if you are a project manager, you need to understand the difference between projects and nonprojects. Projects come in all shapes and sizes. There are two definitions that capture the essence of all projects. One is that a project is a job consisting of multiple tasks that is done one time. It should have well-defined starting and ending times, a defined scope of work, and a budget of some kind.

Another definition, by Dr. J. M. Juran, is that a project is a problem scheduled for solution. This definition supports the previous one, and makes us realize that when we do a project, we are solving a problem for the organization. However, we don't necessarily mean "problem" in a negative sense. Developing a new product is a positive kind of problem. So is moving to a new facility.

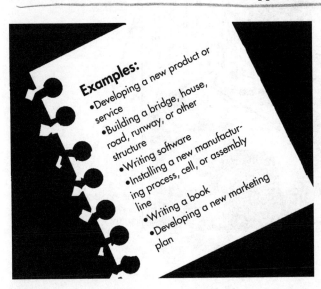

TABLE 2.1   Examples of Projects

Examples:
- Developing a new product or service
- Building a bridge, house, road, runway, or other structure
- Writing software
- Installing a new manufacturing process, cell, or assembly line
- Writing a book
- Developing a new marketing plan

Given these definitions, we find that projects exist in many different disciplines. Table 2.1 lists examples of projects. Table 2.2 provides examples of things that are *not* projects.

If you have any experience managing projects, you no doubt recognize that a lot of so-called projects do not conform to the first definition. Rather than having well-defined starting and end-

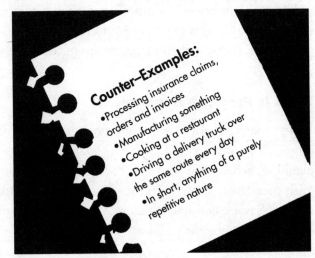

TABLE 2.2   Counter–Examples

Counter-Examples:
- Processing insurance claims, orders and invoices
- Manufacturing something
- Cooking at a restaurant
- Driving a delivery truck over the same route every day
- In short, anything of a purely repetitive nature

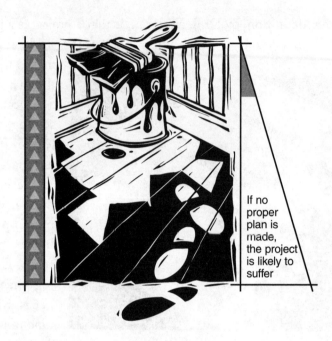

If no proper plan is made, the project is likely to suffer

ing points, they seem to evolve from some vague idea to full-blown project status, and like the Energizer Bunny, they also keep on going and going and going.

The problem caused by a project evolving from a vague idea into a full-blown effort is that proper planning is usually not done. And, if no proper plan is made, then management of the project is likely to suffer.

What Is Project Management?

Project management is really not much more than organized common sense. To be more specific, project management is facilitation of the planning, scheduling, and controlling of activities needed to accomplish objectives. These objectives include cost, performance, time, and scope. They are defined in Figure 2.1. The relationship among them is given by this equation

$$C = f(P, T, S)$$

The equation means, "Cost is a function of Performance, Time, and Scope."

Project managers are always making trade-offs between these four objectives. It is very common that senior managers try to assign values to all four of them, yet we know that in an

Project management is really not much more than organized common sense.

equation with four variables, only three can have values assigned. The fourth will be whatever the equation says it will be. This means that project managers will often have to negotiate with others to establish a balanced cost equation. In many cases earlier commitments of all four objectives will have been made, and unfortunately that negotiation will not happen. The project manager is now placed in a very difficult position. If she says no, she might be accused by senior management of not being a team player. If she says yes, she might set herself up for an

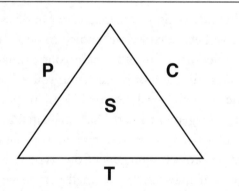

P - At the desired performance level; this is the *quality* objective

C - Within budget (cost)

T - On time (to meet the schedule)

S - While managing the *scope*, or magnitude of project work

FIGURE 2.1   The Four Objectives of Project Management

eventual failure. Although a detailed answer is beyond the scope of this book, the answer lies in formally proposing and prioritizing feasible alternatives from which senior management must pick one. In other words, to simply say yes to an impossible situation is not acceptable. Just make sure it really is an impossible situation and that no amount of creativity will resolve it before you push back to senior management. You are creating a potentially embarrassing position, and you might be the one who is embarrassed.

Types of Project Manager Roles

There are two types of project managers we will consider in this book. They are the occasional project manager and the dedicated or full-time project manager.

The Occasional Project Manager

Most of you will practice project management in this setting. For some of you it will have been a conscious choice to do so, and for others a condition of employment. In either case your primary responsibility will be to a business function or process, and you will use project management as one of many tools to meet your responsibilities. Even though project management is not your principal avocation, it is an important part of what you do. Remember, Tom Peters believes that we will all become project managers of one type or another, and that project management may only be a small part of what we do but it might also be a major part of what we do. In any case, you will want to develop some level of proficiency, so this book will be important to your professional development whatever that level of proficiency might be.

There are no doubt more part-time project managers than there are full-time managers. If you run projects occasionally, the natural question to ask is, "Just how much time should I invest in learning the tools of project management?" Certainly you wouldn't likely want to get a master's degree in project management if you only manage projects occasionally. You might not even want a noncredit certificate. But you should definitely know the essential tools of project management. These include tools for planning, scheduling, and controlling projects. Table 2.3 lists

Tools of Project Management

- Work breakdown structures
- PERT/CPM scheduling
- Gantt or bar chart schedules
- Earned value analysis
- Risk probability numbers

TABLE 2.3   Tools of Project Management

the basic tools that anyone managing projects should be familiar with. Whether you use them regularly is not too important. You can always choose not to use tools that you know, but you can't use tools that you don't know about.

These tools can be learned in a three-day seminar on project management. If you have not had such a course, you should study prospective course outlines to see that they cover these topics. Further, you should be wary of one- and two-day programs that promise to make you a professional project manager. It takes at least three days to cover these methods in detail, since you need practice in applying them. A well-designed program will involve some skill-building exercises that have you apply the tools as you learn them.

You might also want to learn these tools by reading and actively using a good practice-oriented book on project management. For example, you might adopt Bob Wysocki's *Effective Project Management* (Second Edition), or Jim Lewis's book *Project Planning, Scheduling and Control*. Both present project management with an applications and "how-to" approach.

One trap that occasional project managers often confront is that they are expected to be *working* project managers. This means they are expected to perform some of the work that their team members also do. This can be okay on very small projects, but at some point the work will take priority over managing the job, and managing will suffer. When this happens, you need to ask that you be relieved of the work responsibility so that you can concentrate on your managing responsibilities. This does not mean that you will be a full-time project manager forever, but for the duration of this project, it may be necessary. Otherwise, at review time, you will be evaluated on managing, and your supervisor may tell you that your managing leaves something to be desired.

> **. . . project management can be a goal in and of itself as well as an intermediate stop on the way to either consulting or senior management positions.**

One obvious advantage to being an occasional project manager is that you have a chance to see if you want to be a full-time project manager. As is true of any profession, there are pros and cons about project management. Project management does have high visibility in a lot of companies, and offers a bridge between lower level positions and consulting or executive level jobs. In fact, there is some reason to believe that project management may become the route to the top in the future. We discuss a career model later in this chapter that shows how project managers are positioned in a comprehensive career ladder. That model demonstrates how project management can be a goal in and of itself as well as an intermediate stop on the way to either consulting or senior management positions.

However, project managers often suffer a great deal of stress, so "If you can't stand the heat, get out of the kitchen," as the old saying goes. We have found a lot of people who *want to be managers* but don't really *want to manage*. There is a big difference.

If you are an occasional project manager and are trying to make up your mind whether to go for a full-time position, this book should be especially useful. If you are already a full-time project manager, later

Project managers endure a great deal of "stress"

sections of this chapter will help you decide how to use the book to further develop your career.

The Dedicated or Full-time Project Manager

There is a philosophy followed in some organizations that says if you can manage one project, you can manage any project. You might work for this type of organization and find it to be as much, if not more of a challenge than working as an occasional project

One obvious advantage to being an occasional project manager is that you have a chance to see if you want to be a full-time project manager.

manager. Your organization may be structured along the lines of a projectized organization, in which case project managers are dedicated project managers. Organizationally they may be attached to a project office or report to a vice president of projects. They move from project to project. When one project is finished, they are reassigned to another project. Although these projects might be in the same discipline, that is not always the case. That is the job of the dedicated project manager. The dedicated project manager will most often be found in a projectized organization, and we will have more to say about that in Chapter Six. For now we simply recognize the existence of the dedicated project manager.

If you already are a full-time project manager, or aspire to be one, the question would be whether you want to continue in project management for the foreseeable future. If you do, should you get an advanced degree, a certificate, or just continue as you are? This book is designed to help you make these decisions. There are a lot of organizations looking for professional project managers. Some are even insisting that you have Project Management Institute (PMI) certification (not to be confused with a certificate in project management). We will discuss PMI™ certification later in this chapter. A project manager told Jim Lewis recently that he tried to get a job that paid $100,000 a year, but was turned down because he did not have his PMI™ certification. So professional project managers have a bright future at the moment, and this should not change unless there becomes a glut in the market.

The Project Manager Food Chain

Whether you are an occasional or dedicated project manager, there is another way to slice the project manager pie. We introduce that here and leave the details for Chapter Four. There are several stages of professional growth for the project manager. It starts out when you first realized that you wanted to be a project manager. We call these the "wanna-bes" and start them at the entry-level position that we call team member. Chapter Four defines the specific entry-level skill profile that you will need in order to be a team member. As you might guess, this will be a minimal set of project management skills and will encompass mainly personal and interpersonal skills as well as business and general management skills. Team members are generally chosen based on their technical skills rather than on any project manage-

Team members are generally chosen based on their technical skills rather than on any project management skills they might have.

ment skills they might have. As you continue your participation as a team member you will eventually acquire a basic set of project management skills either through on-the-job experience or formal training. This will prepare you to move to the next level, which we call a team leader. This is a fancy name for an individual who manages a piece of work within the project. As team leader you will often have one or two subject matter specialists working with you on an activity within the project. Again in Chapter Four we define the specific entry-level skills that you will need in order to be a team leader. You will have additional assignments as team leader that will move you from simple to more complex types of assignments. Along the way your team size may increase and give you more experience working with larger groups of people on more complex activities. This process repeats itself with additional project management skills acquisition on your part as you move along a defined path from team leader to project manager to senior project manager to program manager. Did you ever expect the career path of the project manager to be this extensive? As you will see, it provides a clearly defined path that will give you a foundation on which to build a sound professional development plan. Depending on your interest in retaining your focus as a technical expert, you may trade off with your project manager aspirations. For example, if you want to be an internal consultant, recognized for your specialization, you might aspire to be a team leader. Your contribution to a project will be to lead a team of others in your area of specialization. This can be a very challenging and rewarding experience for those who want to be a specialist and yet have some involvement with project management.

PMI™ Certification

PMI™ is the major professional association of project managers in the United States. Its membership reached 54,000 in January 2000 and continues to increase at a rate of about 25 percent per year. There is every reason to believe that that growth rate will continue into the forceseeable future. Of those 54,000 members, over 15,000 had achieved certification as a Project Management Professional (PMP™). To achieve this professional certification, an individual has to pass a written exam and demonstrate practice of the profession for a period of two years. The exam tests your knowledge in nine areas, called the Project Management Body of Knowledge (PMBOK™).

TABLE 2.4   The Project Management Body of Knowledge

These areas are shown in Table 2.4. There is also an annual continuing education requirement needed to maintain certification. That can be met by attending conferences or participating in additional seminars and workshops. Many companies are now requiring PMI™ certification as a condition of moving along their project manager career path. You should find out how your company views such certification and what they are willing to do to support employees who are interested in seeking it.

As was stated previously, the PMI™ is the professional association for project managers. They have a program to certify project managers as professionals. The designation that follows your name is PMP™, which means Project Management Professional.

As was mentioned, some companies are requiring that their project managers become certified. Others are insisting that consulting firms must employ PMP™s if they are going to do contracting or consulting for them. For more information on PMP™ certification, contact the PMI™ (see Appendix A). Many of the university certificate programs are designed to help people prepare for the PMP™ certification exam. If you intend to become certified, this would be an important consideration in selecting a certificate program to attend. PMI™ has chapters throughout the United States that offer certification study groups as well, so you can obtain study materials from PMI™ and then attend a study group to prepare for the exam.

The Career Progression Model

To further put the project manager career paths into perspective, we have constructed a model that illustrates the options open to you. Figure 2.2 is the Project Manager Career Progression Model.

The first thing to note about this model is that project management positions are the staging point for either of two career paths. One is a consultant track that allows you to continue working as an individual contributor or team leader but with increasing responsibilities having enterprise-wide scope. The other is a management track that allows you to move farther up in the organization by changing your job focus from the management of work (project manager) to the management of people (general manager). In both cases, however, you should expect to pass through a stage where you have some level of project management responsibility. That responsibility can range anywhere from team leader through program manager. Note also that project management positions are excellent preparation for either of the three further career

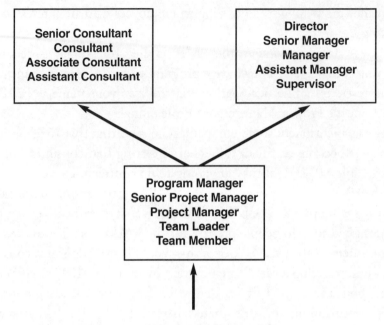

FIGURE 2.2   Project Manager Career Progression Model

paths. During your tenure as a project manager you will discover whether your professional goals lie within project management or whether you aspire to positions as an individual contributor (consultant track) or to positions in people management (management track).

The Good, the Bad, and the Ugly

So far everything sounds pretty good. Would that it were true. We feel compelled at this early stage to tell you that being a project manager is easy, but being a successful project manager is very difficult. It isn't because you are not appropriately skilled for the job but rather because you face a very difficult, ever-changing, and usually hostile environment. This topic is so important that we have devoted an entire chapter to it. We were fortunate to recruit Doug DeCarlo, who at the time was a senior consultant for the ICS Group in Norwalk, Connecticut, to share his expertise on this hostile environment and write Chapter Seven for us. For now it is sufficient to briefly mention that there are

> **... being a project manager is easy, but being a successful project manager is very difficult.**

at least three causes for this hostile environment as discussed below.

Unrealistic Targets

Being competitive in today's fast-paced business world means getting there first, with the best and at the best price. Today's businesses are forced, by nature, to be aggressive, and that aggressiveness translates into project requirements and schedules that are often unrealistic. Someone once said: "If you can't meet the customer's requirements, they will find someone who will." If you expect to succeed as a project manager, you must understand the situation you are placed in and deal with it in the best way possible.

Lack of Resources

One of the realities of downsizing is that many of the people are gone, but somehow their work didn't go away. That means that the survivors are overburdened with work, and this translates into problems for the

project manager. As project manager you do not have line authority over your team members. You simply manage their work,

> **"If you can't meet the customer's requirements, they will find someone who will."**

and this will require sound leadership skills from you. You are in a position of having to influence without authority. Your team members are organizationally accountable to their line manager, who has to deal with several competing and often conflicting requests for their time.

Here the project manager must function as negotiator, and that situation creates uncertainty for them. They never really know when they can count on a resource to be available on the agreed scheduled date and for the agreed level of effort over an agreed length of time. Again, if you expect to succeed as a project manager, you must understand the resource contention problem that you are placed in and deal with it in the best way possible. That will draw upon your skills as a creative problem solver and negotiator.

Is This a Losing Situation?

To be frank, it often is. You may find that discouraging, but that's reality. You will need a firm resolve to be a project manager, and that means you will need to be well-prepared for the battle ahead. We have put into the pages of this book all of the wisdom and experience we have gathered over the thirty-five years that each of us has been involved in project management. That is the best we can do for you. The rest will be up to you.

> **To be frank, it often is.**

Types of Projects

Just as project managers come in all sizes, shapes, and descriptions, so do projects. As we look deeper into the types of projects you will encounter you will realize that they offer you a rich source of development opportunities. There is a natural progression of projects in terms of technical and organizational complexity, and that progression fits neatly into our career progression model for project managers. Make no mistake, there are a number of possibilities for you to tap into as you look for on-the-project training and development opportunities. Let's explore this classification model a bit and leave it to later chapters to dig deeper into the possibilities.

The project classification model we use in this book was originally developed by the Center for Project Management (CPM), a Califor-

nia project management consulting and training company. It is a robust model that defines four types of projects based on an assessment of the projects' organizational and technical complexity (Table 2.5). In Chapter Four we present a mapping of these project types to project manager skill profiles. Using the skill assessment tool found in Appendix B, you will be able to evaluate yourself against these profiles. This establishes the baseline from which we will show you how to plan your own professional development program.

Technically Complex Projects

Technical complexity refers to the technology that will be used in the project. Think of technology in the broadest sense of the term. In other words, engineering, research and development, science,

PROJECT TYPE	TECHNICAL COMPLEXITY	ORGANIZATION COMPLEXITY	PROJECT MANAGER TYPE
IV	Simple	Simple	Team Leader
III	Complex	Moderate	Project Manager
II	Moderate	Complex	Project manager
I	Complex	Complex	Sr. Project Manager Program Manager

TABLE 2.5   Matching Project Type to Project Manager

construction, medicine, the biological sciences, and others are included. If the technology is well established or otherwise in common use in the organization, the project will be classified as simple from a technical standpoint. That means that few problems, if any, will be expected. The project will not be at risk for any technical reasons.

If it is a new technology or is otherwise unfamiliar to the organization, the project will be classified as complex from a technical standpoint. Technical complexity can also arise when a known technology is being applied in a new or unique way. If the staff needed to use the technology are scarce or not fully qualified, that may contribute to the technical complexity. Obviously such projects will be at risk and have a high probability of failure.

Organizationally Complex Projects

Organizational complexity refers to the environment in which the project will be undertaken. If the project involves only one function or unit within the organization, affects only a few processes or procedures, and does not require considerable cultural adjustment or change, it will be classified as organizationally simple. On the other

Technical complexity refers to technology used.

hand, if it represents considerable change, is highly controversial, or affects several processes or procedures, it will be classified as organizationally complex. The stability of the organization will also contribute to organizational complexity.

Summary

At this point we have given you a high level look at projects, project management, and the project manager. You understand that there are two types of project manager, occasional or dedicated, and that each has a very different role in the organization. You also understand that there is a career ladder that progresses to project management and beyond into either consulting or people management. You might choose to have project management as a career goal or use it as a staging area for more professional growth. To give you an even further perspective on being a project manager, the next chapter contains Jim Lewis's interviews of several practicing project managers.

chapter 3

Profiles of Project Managers

Introduction

Project managers can be found everywhere. As pointed out earlier, some were placed in the position, while others chose it voluntarily. Whichever the case, there are a number of situations we would like to bring to your attention as you contemplate possible futures.

Profiles of Project Managers

Just what kind of person makes a good project manager? Is there a way to tell beforehand if you have what it takes, or do you have to spend time finding out the hard way?

We have been asked many times what characteristics we believe are most important for a project manager to have, and have never hesitated to say, "Good people skills." The reason is very simple: Project managers often have considerable responsibility, yet seldom have any authority over the people on their project teams. This means that the only way they will get anything done is through the exercise of influence, persuasion, negotiation, and maybe a little begging at times. So interpersonal skills are at the top of our list.

We have also asked participants in our seminars to list the qualities they want to see in a project manager, and the following table shows what they consistently say.

Attributes of Project Managers

Good listener	Mutual ownership
Supportive	Buffer to rest of organization
Organized	Visible leadership
Clears roadblocks	Technical knowledgeb
Mutual respect	Fair
Team builder	Flexible
Knows own limitations	Open-minded
Sense of humor	Delegates
Gives feedback	Honest and trustworthy
Good decision maker	Understanding
Follows up	Challenges team to do well
Shares experience	Knows strengths and weaknesses of team members

---

 Notice the small number of items in the list that have to do with the technical and administrative aspects of project management. These are not top priorities for people. Rather, what is important to them is what we would call the *character* of the manager. She is trustworthy, shows mutual respect for co-workers, is a good listener, and so on. Without these qualities, people are not eager to follow your lead, and a project manager must be a leader of the team.

The HBDI and Project Managers

Elsewhere we have discussed the Herrmann Brain Dominance Instrument (HBDI), which measures thinking preferences. We wondered what kind of profile would be typical for project managers, so we asked the Herrmann International people to pull the profiles of all the project managers they had in their database. They had 1,250 profiles

Project managers can be found everywhere.

of people who reported being project coordinators (the official title used by Herrmann International to classify this occupation). The overall average profile for the group was almost perfectly square.

What does that tell us? It says that the kind of people who become project managers come in all shapes and sizes (profile-wise). Some are conceptual thinkers. Some love doing detail work. Some are analytical, and some are more interpersonal. There is no dominant profile that says "this person will be an ideal project manager."

In fact, you can see that thinking in all four quadrants is necessary in managing a project. When you are developing project strategy, you need conceptual thinking (yellow, or the D-Quadrant). When you start developing an implementation plan, you need green, or B-Quadrant thinking. During execution you have to deal with lots of people issues, which requires red, or C-Quadrant thinking. And when prob-

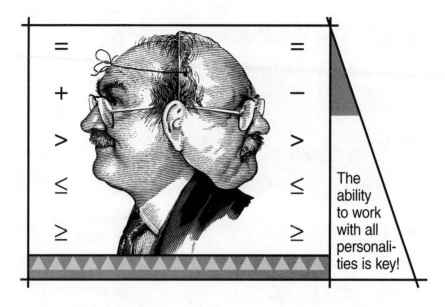

lems exist, you may need a good shot of analytical thinking (blue, or the B-Quadrant).

Ned Herrmann suggested that good chief executive officers could benefit by having square profiles, because this would make them better able to translate between the quadrants. This is important, since they have to deal with people in all four quadrants.

We believe the same can be said for project managers. You have to deal with people whose thinking preferences fall in all four quadrants, so it would be nice to have a balanced profile yourself.

Most of us aren't that lucky. So we have to cover those quadrants where we have low preferences by making sure someone on our team does the thinking required—or else we have to force ourselves to do the required thinking, even though it is not our strong preference. Remember—we all have a whole brain, we just prefer to exercise certain modes of thinking more than others. It's not that we can't do it; it's just that we don't prefer some modes.

Interviews with Project Managers

To help you get a better picture of what it means to be a project manager, we have interviewed five project managers from different walks of life. The summaries of those interviews are given below.

A Manager of Project Managers

In preparing this book, we interviewed a number of managers of project managers and asked them this question: "What do you consider important characteristics of a good project manager?" The responses we received are as follows.

George Hollins is director of design and construction services at the University of Iowa, in Iowa City. George did not hesitate to respond.

> **"People skills! We give our biggest and most important projects to the project managers who can deal best with people."**

"People skills! We give our biggest and most important projects to the project managers who can deal best with people. We sometimes think that a person who is a really good architect will be a good project manager, but it isn't necessarily true."

He said they actually had to take one fellow out of the project management job and put him back into a technical job because he had a way of irritating people with whom he dealt. And that included not only members of the project team, but customers as well. "He just didn't know how to get along with people," said Hollins.

George himself first earned a degree in civil engineering, then went on to get a degree in business administration. He considers project management to be a key to the success of the projects they manage, which are to build classroom buildings for the university. He has invested heavily in training his staff in those principles. He plans to get his PMP^{tm} in the near future.

A Long-time Project Manager

Bob Dudley managed projects in paper mills for nearly thirty years before he retired recently. He was also an operations manager for about six years, so he has seen "both sides of the fence." Bob earned a degree from the University of Florida in construction, but scheduling by using the critical path method was fairly new at the time, so he had to learn much of it later on the job. Before he retired, he passed his PMP™ certification, because he views project management as his profession. He now consults on and teaches project management.

> **"People skills are numbers one and two."**

Bob says, "You have to look at a project as an integrated whole. Many project managers are either estimators or schedulers, and they forget the big picture." He added, "Communication skills are of utmost importance. Some of the project managers I have known can't write a coherent sentence."

"People skills are numbers one and two," he said. "You can't get the cooperation of superintendents, mechanics, and other people affected by the project without them. You also need a field presence. You need to know what you're talking about. You can't b.s. them. And you can't run a project from an office. You have to get into the field."

> **"... you can't run a project from an office. You have to get into the field."**

He went on to tell about a project manager who was having trouble getting people to come to meetings to sign drawing changes. He started taking a box of doughnuts and a big pot of coffee to the superintendent's office for the Tuesday morning meeting. People started coming in.

As Bob said, it might seem trivial, but the project manager did something that showed a willingness to give them something in return for their help, and they responded by giving that help.

An Engineering Project Manager

Harold Arnison has a BS in industrial technology and has worked as an electrical engineer for eighteen years, doing product development. Those products are medical electronics, which require FDA approval and so must be of the highest caliber.

The company he works for was recently acquired by General Electric, one of the few companies that has a dual career ladder. Before the acquisition, however, Harold earned his master's in project management from Kellogg Graduate School, because he was intrigued by the discipline and wanted to improve his skills. He is now an adviser of project managers. He plans to get his PMP™ certification soon.

"The ability to work with people of all personalities is a key competency," Harold said. "We have to work with very diverse groups. We have people with medical degrees, technical degrees, and no degrees at all, and we must be able to work smoothly with them."

He went on to say that a project manager must have a structured approach to his or her work. They must be able to develop a good plan, yet remain flexible so that they can "roll with inevitable changes" that affect every project. "They have to be able to develop a schedule for unscheduled events," he added, and he emphasized that "these are far easier to deal with if you have a plan in the first place."

> **"The ability to work with people of all persuasions is a key competency."**

He said, "Everything we do is under project management control. However, we don't use money as a metric as much as we should, but we are going that way." He was referring to earned value tracking.

His advice to wanna-be project managers: "Realize that you must leave your technical skills alone. Don't take on a significant part of design work. If you do, you fall into the managing-versus-doing trap, and the managing always suffers."

An Example from India

A few years ago, Jim Lewis was in India teaching project management, and a participant told him this story. It seems that a large road construction project was having serious problems. Working conditions were bad, the food the workers were fed was substandard, and living conditions at the site were abominable. (The workers lived in tents at the construction site, as it was in a remote location.) The result was that morale was low, motivation was nonexistent, and work was going at a snail's pace.

The project manager and his assistants stayed at a nice hotel in a town some distance from the site, and commuted back and forth. This added to the low morale of workers. Fortunately, the project manager figured out what was wrong and took steps to correct the problem. He moved to the site, together with his assistants. Living conditions for the workers quickly improved. The food improved. And with it came an improvement in worker morale, motivation, and performance.

A Young Female Project Manager

Carol asked not to be identified, but gave us permission to include her comments as follows. She is twenty-five years old, an engineer, and is managing a project in which her team is in the Northeast, whereas she is located in the Southeast. In managing this high-tech project, she had two strikes against her. First, the team is at a remote location. Second, because of her age and gender, they saw her as an interference, or perhaps even worse, as a threat. In any case, things did not go well at the beginning.

Carol explained that she simply visited the team monthly to let them know that she was not there to interfere with their work, or to direct them in how to do it, but to be a resource for them. If there was anything they needed, she would do her best to get it for them.

After several months of approaching them in this way, they began to accept her, and in the end they fully accepted her role as the project manager. Had she not won them over by adopting the helper or facilitator role, she may never have been successful in managing the project.

This example again illustrates the need for dealing with the human side of the equation. Her expertise as an engineer counted for very little. It let them know that she at least could understand their work, but that was all. Furthermore, her role as project manager was initially rejected, and her attempt to plan, schedule, and control the project never would have worked if she hadn't gained their acceptance of her. What is significant is that Carol actually exercised the attributes of a leader to win over the members of this team.

"They Don't Know How to Manage Projects"

We interviewed Julian Stubbs, CEO of the Dowell//Stubbs advertising agency, located in Stockholm, about project management in an ad agency. "I'm having a terrible time finding project managers," Julian said. "I can find plenty of individuals who have good technical skills. They can do artwork, write copy, and manage accounts, but they don't know how to manage projects."

We asked him what he considers to be vital skills for project managers in an ad agency. His reply was immediate: "To be able to manage chaos, to respond to quick turnaround requests, to meet deadlines, and to smooth ruffled feathers." He went on: "Egos in advertising and marketing people can be pretty high, and they don't always take kindly to being 'managed' in the first place. If you don't deal with them with kid gloves, you will never get the job done."

Julian went on to say that they don't do highly structured scheduling, using PERT/CPM techniques, but every project is deadline driven, and because of the creative nature of the work, it is always tempting for people to say that it is hard to meet deadlines, but it is mandatory, and creativity can't be sacrificed in the process. The pressure can be enormous, and only a person who can deal with that pressure will be successful in such an environment.

Interview Questions

Following are some of the kinds of questions that are asked of project manager candidates. You should find these helpful in thinking about your own qualifications. They will also help you prepare for an upcoming interview.

- What does project management mean to you?
- What was a valuable lesson you learned from a project, and how did you (or will you) apply it to future projects?
- What do you do to handle conflicts within a project team?
- Tell us about one success and one failure you've had on projects.
- Why do you feel you're qualified for this position?
- How would you handle a project that's offtrack or stalled?
- What characteristics do you bring to this position?
- How do you deal with a non-team player or difficult team member?
- If priorities change, what do you do?
- How do you see yourself in the role of project manager?
- What do you do when there is a conflict about the P, C, T, S targets?
- How would you handle misinformation from team members?
- Describe what a successful project is.
- Suppose there is a change in expectations of a key stakeholder to your project. What would you do?
- What do you do when you feel that senior management is setting unobtainable project goals?
- In a project in which team efforts seem to be heading in the wrong direction, what actions would you take to correct the situation?

Summary

The message must be clear by now: Technical skills are less important than the ability to deal effectively with people, regardless of the field you are in. That doesn't mean that you can manage projects that you

You must be able to communicate.

▶Communicate
▶Negotiate
▶Lead
▶Influence
▶Manage Conflict
▶Deal with Politics

know nothing about. Remember, you can't b.s. field people—or engineers or scientists, or programmers. However, you need not be a technical expert; nor can you be on a multidisciplinary project.

You must be able to communicate, negotiate, lead, influence, manage conflict, and deal with politics. You have to understand people. And you need to care about them. If you don't care about people, they will sense it, and will not readily go the extra mile for you.

Jim once had an engineer ask him, "I understand that if you're going to be a good manager, you're supposed to take an interest in the people in your team. You're supposed to ask, 'How's the wife? How's the kid? How's the family dog?'"

Jim agreed.

"But I don't care about any of that stuff," he said. "What am I supposed to do?"

"Don't be a manager," Jim said.

"I thought so," he said. "But my boss wants me to be one, so I've been trying to keep an open mind."

He was a techie. He loved technology. And he hated having to deal with "small talk" and the personal issues of his team members. He should never be a manager, because he hated doing the very things that make managers effective.

So ask yourself, "Do I like dealing with 'people problems'? Do I enjoy trying to get people motivated? Do I find it challenging to get the best out of team members?"

Unless you can answer yes to these questions, forget project management as a career, close the book, and pass it on to a friend who is soul-searching just as you are.

chapter 4

Do You Want to Be
a Project Manager?

Introduction

As glamorous as you might want to think the job of a project manager is, let us be very clear about what it entails. Yes, it is a position of great visibility. And yes, it is a position that can bring great rewards. But it is also a position that carries great risk because of all the unknowns that can rise up unexpectedly and bring disaster to even the best of plans. In this chapter we take a very close look at the various positions that are part of the career ladder of the project manager. We will start at the bottom of the project manager "food chain" and describe the positions that you can expect to occupy as you make your way to the top— or maybe we should say as you make your way to whatever you have decided will be the top for you.

This is the decision chapter for you. By the time you have completed this chapter you should have decided whether you want to be a project manager and, if so, what type of project manager you want to be. You might also be able to see beyond the position of project manager into further career progression, in either consulting or general management.

A project manager position is a position of great visibility and great risk.

What Is a Project Manager?

Simply stated, a project manager is a person who is responsible for completing a defined piece of work within an established budget, by a specific date, and with a defined set of resources (people, equipment, and facilities). Simple to say, but oh so difficult to attain. It would be simple if the work, once defined, didn't change, and if the delivery date, once set, didn't change, and if the resources, once committed, were available. But that isn't going to happen, so that is where the challenge of being a successful project manager takes its cue. We have often heard project managers say that it would be a boring job if these things didn't change, but the fact that they do change is what gets them out of bed in the morning. You can't have it both ways!

What Does a Project Manager Do?

To get a good understanding of what a project manager does, we will define five types of positions on project teams. These five positions form a career path starting at the entry level and progressing to the most experienced and seasoned project management professional. Each of the five types has defined roles and responsibilities, which we will discuss in this section. We will leave for later sections the discussion of the skills needed to fulfill these roles and responsibilities.

A Team Member

For most of you, your career as a project manager will begin as a team member. At the entry level you possess some skill that is needed by the project team, and that is the reason why you have been selected as a team member. For example: You are working on a project management methodology development project, and your team is responsible for designing and developing the training curriculum that will be needed. Your job as a member of this team is to develop the slide presentation that accompa-

To meet your team member responsibilities, you will need a very fundamental understanding of project management only in that you have an obligation to provide periodic status information to either your team leader or to the project manager.

nies the courses. That is all you are responsible for, and when you have finished and your work has been approved, you will have met your responsibility to the curriculum development team and will leave the project. During the times that you are actually doing work for the project, you will work under the direction of a team leader or project manager. You might be involved with the project for its entire duration, or be active only for a brief time as you deliver the work you have been asked to do.

During the time you are working on the project, you might be committed full-time or for only a percentage of your time. You can also expect to be assigned to more than one project at a time. To meet your team member responsibilities, you will need a very fundamental understanding of project management only in that you have an obligation to provide periodic status information to either your team leader or to the project manager. How to do that is something you can learn on the job. There is no requirement for formal training in project management at this point. However, in anticipation of becoming a team leader someday, you should begin reading about project management at an introductory level and maybe even look into taking a three-day introductory course. If you can do that, when the time comes you will be prepared to move to team leader. Keep in mind, however, that a person moves to team leader responsibility based more on their on-the-job performance and recommendations of their team leader than on any formal training.

> ... a person moves to team leader responsibility based more on their on-the-job performance and recommendations of their team leader than on any formal training.

A Team Leader

As you gain experience as a team member you will increase your skills through on-the-project experience and perhaps some formal training in project management at an introductory level. That will prepare you to take on limited responsibility for the work of a small team within a larger project. At the entry level you can expect team size to consist of only a few members whose expertise lies within a limited scope of work. As you learn how to direct the work of a few on a simple task, you can expect to expand to larger teams with a broader and more complex range of responsibilities.

Team leaders get good on-the-job training in project management in a somewhat protected environment. To a great extent they are insulated from the environment by the project manager. That allows them

As you gain experience as a team member, you will increase your skills.

to focus on the specific activity for which they are responsible. Changes are negotiated by the project manager, and they are simply the recipient of those changes even though they may have had some role in deciding if and how to handle those changes. While you serve as team leader you can focus on learning what we call the "block and tackle" of project

Team leaders get good on-the-job training in project management in a somewhat protected environment.

management. That is, you can focus on learning how to use the tools and techniques, leaving change management, politics, and communications with the stakeholders to the project manager. You will learn about project scoping, project planning (the work breakdown structure; estimating activity duration, resources, and cost; scheduling project work), reporting project progress, closing the project, and conducting a post-project audit.

Given enough broadening experiences as well as formal training in project management, you will eventually reach a skill level that prepares you for an entry-level project manager position. Here you step up to a new set of challenges. Those aspects that were external to the work of the project that were the province of the project manager are now on your plate. Let's take a look at what that means.

A Project Manager

To be effective your interpersonal relations, which include problem solving, decision making, and conflict resolution, are now part of your responsibility. In other words, as a team leader you could focus internally on the project, but now, as a project manager, you have to focus also on the external aspects of the project.

> ... as a team leader you could focus internally on the project, but now, as a project manager, you have to focus also on the external aspects of the project.

At the entry level you can expect to manage projects of limited scope and complexity and impact on the business. Such projects require a manager to have a moderate level of proficiency—technical and business skills in particular—in order to be successful. At the entry level you can expect to have total management responsibility for these projects. As part of your development as a project manager you will need some training. The training is not technical, however. It is more interpersonal. Course titles such as managing diversity in the workplace; how to negotiate to a win-win conclusion; managing technical people; creative problem solving; decision making; and others will be ones you should look for.

The major change that you will notice, as compared with your responsibilities as a team leader, will be the added focus external to the project. You now have direct contact with the customer, resource managers, senior management, vendors, and external contractors. Your involvement will be more managerial than technical, however. Although you may have had similar involvement as a team leader, it was probably of a limited scope and was more technical than managerial.

A Senior Project Manager

At this level you are working on more complex projects that have higher visibility in the organization. Expect to leave some of your technical skills on the side, replacing them with more managerial skills. You may have done some project work as a project manager, but that will decrease as you move into the mainstream as a senior project manager. As your skill profile builds to encompass projects that are either more technical or more organizationally focused, you will take on projects of greater scope and complexity.

At the single project level you have made it once you reach senior project manager status. The organization depends on you to show leadership in the most

The organization depends on you to show leadership in the most difficult of project situations. Younger, less experienced project managers will look to you for advice and counsel.

difficult of project situations. Younger, less experienced project managers will look to you for advice and counsel. You will be mentor to many of them.

A Program Manager

The distinguishing feature in this class of project manager is that program managers oversee other project managers. They will also manage the most challenging of projects in the organization. At this point in your career you have left all technical skills behind and are now a fully vested senior manager in your business unit. You are expected to contribute to the business in a proactive way within the scope of your functional responsibility. This is clearly the territory of the WOW Project.

What Kinds of Projects Do They Manage?

> **You are expected to contribute to the business in a proactive way within the scope of your functional responsibility.**

In Chapter Two we briefly introduced the four types of projects we will use in developing career paths for project managers. As you saw in Table 2.5, each type is distinguished from the others by the level of technical and organizational complexity involved.

Type IV — Simple

Early in your career as a project manager you can expect to start with projects that are relatively straightforward, do not involve complex technologies, and have limited organizational value. For example, the installation of a server network in a field sales office, because it has been done many times over and has become rather routine, is a Type IV project. Projects such as these may seem to offer little in the way of challenge and excitement, but don't be too premature in judging them. As a beginning project manager you will have plenty of challenges and opportunities to grow and learn from such projects.

Type III — Organizationally Complex

These projects tend to use established and current technology but present a rather complex organizational environment. The complexity may arise from the fact that the project affects several business functions, is a new initiative for the enterprise, or is a combination of the two. As an example, consider the merger of two similar companies, such as two banks. The project involves establishing a standardized customer services department that will service the customers of both banks. Each bank has its own way of doing things, and it is your job to get them to agree to a single process. Sound simple? It is not. Pride of ownership and other territorial interests will have to be taken into account. As project manager you will be challenged in ways that you may never have expected.

Type II—Technically Complex

These projects are important to the enterprise but are characterized more on their technological complexity than on their organizational value. Technological complexity can arise in several ways. First, it may be a new technology or at least new to the enterprise. In any case, the enterprise does not have much experience working with it and therefore may only have a small core of professionals who understand it. The risk attendant to such projects obviously will be high. Second, the enterprise could be comfortable with the technology but not have an adequate supply of staff who understands it. A good example of this is an e-business that has companies vying to create its web site. These development efforts challenge the established processes of project management because the systems development method used on these projects is not amenable to standard project management life cycle processes. New ways of thinking about projects and development of an application that is adaptive and constantly changing are needed. These projects are clearly Type II projects.

Type I—Critical Mission

Critical mission projects tend to be on the cutting edge of technology, and a significant contributor to the business's bottom line. For both their technology and their organizational complexities, these projects demand the very best of performance from the very best project managers. As organizations struggle to redefine themselves and their businesses with new technologies driving this change every few years, they are frequently engaging in Type I projects.

What Are Your Career Choices?

Apart from being an occasional or a dedicated project manager, there are general career paths you should be familiar with. These are described below.

The Technical Track

The technical track includes such areas as construction, engineering, science, research and development, and information technology. To be a successful project manager in any of these specialty areas requires, as a minimum, an understanding of the terminology and, in most cases, a working knowledge of the field. It will not, however, generally require current practice of the technical specialty.

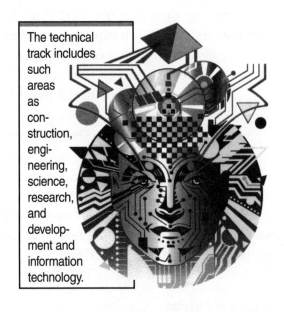

The technical track includes such areas as construction, engineering, science, research, and development and information technology.

The area of information technology is so critical to every business activity that it deserves special mention here. Because we all live and work in the information age, information technology and information systems are the foundation of literally every business or organizational activity in which you might

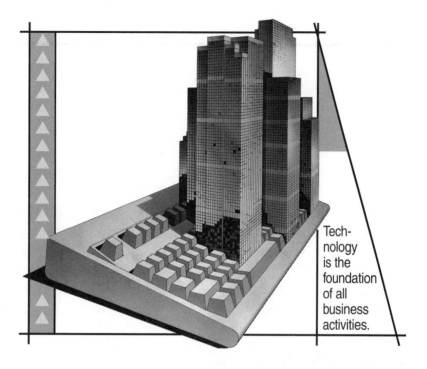

Tech-
nology
is the
foundation
of all
business
activities.

be involved. That means that most projects will include an information technology component regardless of the business function or process involved. The project manager who chooses to have an information technology focus can be assured of levels of project involvement that span all four of the project types discussed earlier.

Furthermore, you are more likely to find the positions of dedicated project manager in the technical track than in the business or management tracks. This is especially true in government-related businesses and projectized organizations.

The Business Track

Within the business functions and organizational processes, the practice of project management is not as widespread as it is in the technical track. The occasional project manager is typically found here, while the dedicated project manager would be a rarity. The area of product development is fertile ground for project management. The need to shorten time to market is a need that can be met with good project management practices.

The Management Track

Many of you are destined to rise above the rank of project manager and become a manager of project managers. This will be the case for dedicated project managers who work in projectized organizations or organizations that staff a project support office with project managers. The strong matrix structure will also have a position such as vice president of projects. All of these are opportunities for those who wish to manage project managers and have a directive responsibility for the project portfolio of the enterprise.

The Demand for Project Managers

As of this writing it is safe to say that the demand for project managers far exceeds the supply of qualified project managers. It is also safe to say that this situation will persist into the foreseeable future. Check out the classified ads section of any major metropolitan newspaper and it will be immediately obvious that project managers are in a seller's market. More recently, companies are posting position openings on their web sites. If you have a project manager career goal in mind and are interested in certain companies, check their web site. PMI® has a rather extensive listing of project manager position openings in a number of companies and geographic areas as well.

PMI® also publishes an annual salary survey. At the time of this writing, its most recent survey was from 1996. In that survey, the reported salary range was $50,000 to over $150,000. Obviously the range includes all levels of experience, industry, and location variables. If you are interested in more details, copies of that survey may be obtained from PMI®.

What Skills Do They Need?

In preparation for our discussion of the skills required to be a world class project manager, let us first look at the functions and tasks that any one of our four project manager types may be called upon to perform.

I. Planning the Project (Strategies and Tactics)

- Develops preliminary study with project team, identifying business problems, requirements, project scope, and benefits
- Identifies key project results and milestones
- Facilitates preparation of project plan and work breakdown structure
- Facilitates the estimation of time lines and project phases

II. Managing the Project

- Continually reviews project status
- Reviews work against key results criteria
- Uses systematic method for logging project status—checking against schedule
- Uses change management/request procedure
- Uses project meetings to measure progress against plan, and communicate changes and issues
- Assesses skill-needed documentation of meetings, work, conversations, and decisions
- Measures quality through testing against requirements
- Conducts project reviews and walk-throughs (with appropriate client involvement)

III. Leading the Project Team

- Involves team in planning
- Uses both formal and informal methods to track project status

- Recognizes individual and team accomplishments or results
- Manages performance issues in a timely manner
- Delegates tasks effectively based on understanding individual strengths and weaknesses
- Maintains open door for staff ideas and concerns

IV. Building Client Partnerships

- Involves working jointly with client in defining project goals and key results
- Works with client to assure alignment of project to overall business goals
- Listens and responds actively, and documents client needs, changes, and demands
- Implements procedures for controlling and handling change
- Develops client understanding of the system and trains in systems use
- Presents and reports periodically to client
- Establishes lines of responsibility and accountability to client

V. Targeting to the Business

- Manages in accordance with visions and values
- Links overall architecture principles
- Interfaces effectively with business systems and processes
- Plans for impacts on related systems/departments to achieve maximum efficiency
- Understands business needs, time, and cost pressures
- Keeps current with business and technology developments in competitors
- Aligns project with corporate and business priorities and direction

Competencies and Skills of the World Class Project Manager

If anyone has a foolproof method of identifying a professional who will make a competent project manager, please contact us. We can show you how to make a lot of money. In fact, it is very difficult to identify someone with the requisite competencies. Figure 4.1 illustrates the difficulty. There are two levels of characteristics that determine success or failure as a project manager. At the visible level are skills, whose level of mastery can be measured, and which can be acquired through training. That is the easy part. More difficult are those traits (competencies) that lie below the surface, out of visible range. We can see them in practice, but we cannot directly measure them in the sense of determining whether or not a particular person has them and, if so, to what degree. They are also the traits that are more difficult to develop through training. Some of them, in fact, may be hereditary.

According to Lyle M. Spencer and Signe M. Spencer's book *Competence at Work: Models for Superior Performance* (New York: John Wiley & Sons, © 1993), a competency is "an underlying characteristic of an individual that is causally related to criterion-referenced effective and/or superior performance in a job or situation." In this book, five types of competency characteristics are identified. These are listed below and briefly explained.

Competency Characteristics

Motives. Those things that a person wants that will cause them to take one course of action rather than another.

Traits. Traits are characteristics that a person possesses that cause him to respond in the manner he does.

Self-Concept. Here we speak of the image that a person has of himself. Values and attitudes are a large part of a person's self-concept.

Knowledge. The awareness, data, and information that a person possesses about a specific topic or content area.

Skill. The observable and measurable performance of an individual to execute an assigned task.

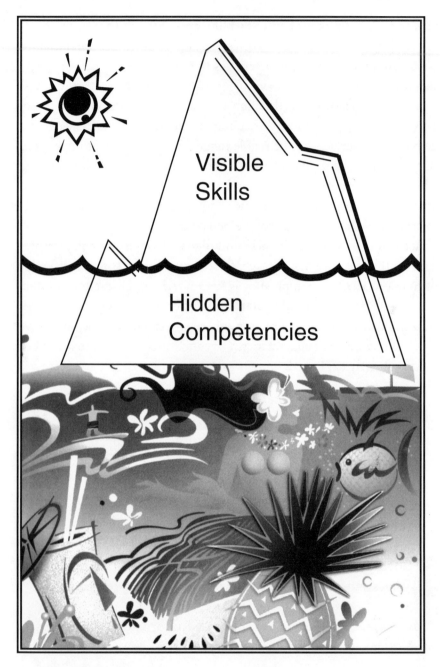

FIGURE 4.1 Project Manager Competencies and Skills

Bob Wysocki's company, Enterprise Information Insights (EII), uses an assessment tool to measure competency in eighteen different areas based on a set of observable behaviors that are related to the competencies. To establish an individual's competency level, we recommend a self-assessment be done by the individual and that several of his coworkers also provide their assessment of the individual. These coworkers might be the individual's manager, peer professionals, subordinates, and customers. Using this approach, the individual's self-assessment can be compared with their coworkers' assessments. This approach may be simplistic, but it is practical and has surfaced rather insightful conclusions regarding individual performance.

For competency assessment we define business, personal, interpersonal, and management categories. Skill assessment adds project management skills as a fifth category. Effective project managers require competencies and skills that are specific to the discipline in which the project they manage lies, and they require a set of non-discipline-specific skills that are categorized into one of the five categories described below.

Business

These competencies and skills relate to the business and business processes in general and do not involve specific business function knowledge.

Personal

Competencies and skills in this category relate to the individual. The skills do not involve another party in order to be practiced.

Interpersonal

Competencies and skills in this category relate to the individual. The skills involve at least two people, neither one of which is the manager of the other.

Management

These competencies and skills relate to all aspects of management, whether people management or work management. Also included are skills related to the performance of strategic and tactical management functions not specific to any individual.

Project Management

Project management skills span the five phases of project management: initiation, planning, organizing, controlling, and closing.

Competency Profile of the World Class Project Manager

This section discusses the competencies common to all levels of project manager. It is meant to give you a general sense of what is required to be an effective project manager and to match your current competencies against those that are required of world class project managers. What results from this examination is a gap between the competencies you have and those that you will need to add to your profile as you move through the ranks of increasing project management responsibility.

Tables 4.1 through 4.4 provide capsule descriptions of the business, personal, interpersonal, and management competencies required to be an effective project manager. As we begin, it would be a good exercise to review this list and personally assess how your competencies measure up. The list was originally developed by the Corporate Education Center of Boston University in cooperation with several of their major corporate accounts. It has since been revised through experience with several other clients and has been adapted here with permission.

It is given here in a survey format so that you can evaluate the extent to which you practice each competency. The rating scale is 5 = Strongly Agree; 4 = Agree; 3 = Neutral; 2 = Disagree; and 1 = Strongly Disagree. Evaluate yourself on each of the competencies and follow the summary instructions given at the end.

Business Competencies

Business Awareness
Ensures that the project is linked to the organization's
business plan and satisfies a business objective
by solving a business problem.   5 4 3 2 1

Evaluates the impact of industry and
technology developments.   5 4 3 2 1

Balances ideal technical approaches and project
scope against business deadlines and priorities
to find the best compromise.   5 4 3 2 1

Quickly adapts to changing business conditions.   5 4 3 2 1

TOTAL BUSINESS AWARENESS SCORE [   ]

Business Partnership
Follows up with business partners, throughout
the cycle of the project, to ensure full understanding
of the business partners' needs and concerns.   5 4 3 2 1

Seeks meaningful business area participation
during the design process.   5 4 3 2 1

Conducts business-oriented walk-throughs.   5 4 3 2 1

Structures the activities of the project team, so that
systems staff work closely with a business partner.   5 4 3 2 1

TOTAL BUSINESS PARTNERSHIP SCORE [   ]

Commitment to Quality
Pushes for more efficient ways to do things.   5 4 3 2 1

Sets and enforces high standards of quality
for self and others.   5 4 3 2 1

Develops a quality plan coordinated with
the project plan.   5 4 3 2 1

Monitors performance against quality plan
and objectives.   5 4 3 2 1

TOTAL COMMITMENT TO QUALITY SCORE [   ]

TABLE 4.1   Business Competencies

68

Personal Competencies

Initiative

Develops innovative and creative approaches to
problems when faced with obstacles or limitations.   5 4 3 2 1

Takes calculated risks.   5 4 3 2 1

Takes persistent action to overcome obstacles
and achieve solutions.   5 4 3 2 1

Puts in whatever effort is needed to get job done.   5 4 3 2 1

TOTAL INITIATIVE SCORE [ ]

Information Gathering

Actively solicits input from all groups that may
be affected by the project.   5 4 3 2 1

Seeks information or data from various
sources to clarify a problem.   5 4 3 2 1

Identifies and consults individuals and groups
that can expedite project activities or provide
assistance.   5 4 3 2 1

Gets enough information to support design and
implementation decisions.   5 4 3 2 1

TOTAL INFORMATION GATHERING SCORE [ ]

Analytic Thinking

Develops an overall project plan including
resources, budget, and time.   5 4 3 2 1

Translates business goals into project goals
and project goals into detailed work breakdown
structures.   5 4 3 2 1

Uses project management software to develop
plans and track status.   5 4 3 2 1

Generates and presents logical, clearly
reasoned alternatives.   5 4 3 2 1

TOTAL ANALYTIC THINKING SCORE [ ]

TABLE 4.2a   Personal Competencies

Personal Competencies (continued)

Conceptual Thinking

Considers the project within the context of a broader view of how the business and technology will be changing over the next several years.	5	4	3	2	1
Uses understanding of business and technical objectives to prioritize effectively (for example: project tasks, test cases, issues to be resolved).	5	4	3	2	1
Anticipates and plans for the impact of the project on other systems.	5	4	3	2	1
Develops a clear vision or conceptual model of the deliverables.	5	4	3	2	1

TOTAL CONCEPTUAL THINKING SCORE [   ]

Self Confidence

Presents a confident and positive attitude to set the tone for the team.	5	4	3	2	1
Confronts problems with others quickly and directly.	5	4	3	2	1
Controls own feelings and behavior in stressful situations.	5	4	3	2	1
Works effectively under pressure.	5	4	3	2	1

TOTAL SELF CONFIDENCE SCORE [   ]

Concern for Credibility

Maintains credibility by consistently delivering what has been promised.	5	4	3	2	1
Stays on top of the details of the project effort, to be able to answer questions authoritatively and maintain credibility.	5	4	3	2	1
Answers questions honestly, even if awkward to do so.	5	4	3	2	1
Promptly informs management and the customer about any difficulties.	5	4	3	2	1

TOTAL CONCERN FOR CREDIBILITY SCORE [   ]

Flexibility

Adjusts readily to changes in the work environment.	5	4	3	2	1
Adjusts own managerial style, depending on the people and situation.	5	4	3	2	1
Uses or shares resources to best accomplish organizational goals.	5	4	3	2	1
Delegates tasks and activities to others.	5	4	3	2	1

TOTAL FLEXIBILITY SCORE [   ]

TABLE 4.2b   Personal Competencies

Interpersonal Competencies

Interpersonal Awareness

Tries to know team members, to understand
what motivates them.   5 4 3 2 1

Understands the issues and concerns of other
individuals and groups.   5 4 3 2 1

Notices and interprets non-verbal behavior.   5 4 3 2 1

Is objective when mediating conflicting positions of
team members.   5 4 3 2 1

TOTAL INTERPERSONAL AWARENESS SCORE ☐

Organizational Awareness

Identifies and seeks the support of key stakeholders.   5 4 3 2 1

Proactively engages groups and individuals with
technical and/or financial overseeing responsibilities. 5 4 3 2 1

Takes the time to understand and consider the political
dynamics among groups involved in the project.   5 4 3 2 1

Uses relationships with people from other units within the
organization to resolve issues or provide assistance.   5 4 3 2 1

TOTAL ORGANIZATIONAL AWARENESS SCORE ☐

Anticipation of Impact

Adapts style or approach to achieve a particular impact. 5 4 3 2 1

Manages expectations by ensuring that what is
promised can be delivered.   5 4 3 2 1

Arranges for a senior manager to attend the initial project
meeting and explain the project's mission and objectives. 5 4 3 2 1

Considers the short and long term implications of
project decisions.   5 4 3 2 1

TOTAL ANTICIPATION OF IMPACT SCORE ☐

Resourceful use of Influence

Develops strategies that address other people's
most important concerns.   5 4 3 2 1

Enlists the support of his/her management to
influence other managers.   5 4 3 2 1

Enlists cooperation by appealing to people's unique expertise. 5 4 3 2 1

Involves project team members in the detail planning
of the project, so they will have ownership of the plan. 5 4 3 2 1

TOTAL RESOURCEFUL USE OF INFLUENCE SCORE ☐

TABLE 4.3 Interpersonal Competencies

Management Competencies

Motivating Others

Ensures that team members understand the project's goals and purpose.	5 4 3 2 1
Provides rewards and recognition to people as milestones are reached.	5 4 3 2 1
Initiates informal events to promote team work.	5 4 3 2 1
Takes appropriate action to assist and counsel marginal performers.	5 4 3 2 1

TOTAL MOTIVATING OTHERS SCORE [   ]

Communications

Organizes and meets regularly with a management team composed of representatives from all areas affected by the project.	5 4 3 2 1
Plans and holds regular, frequent meetings with the project team to discuss status, resolve issues and share information.	5 4 3 2 1
Ensures that presentations are well-organized.	5 4 3 2 1
Tailors his/her language to the level of the audience.	5 4 3 2 1

TOTAL COMMUNICATIONS SCORE [   ]

Developing Others

Gives team members assignments or training to provide opportunities for growth and development.	5 4 3 2 1
Provides direct, specific, constructive feedback and guidance to others regarding their performance.	5 4 3 2 1
Empowers team members to create challenge and stretch their abilities.	5 4 3 2 1
Provides closer supervision for inexperienced people.	5 4 3 2 1

TOTAL DEVELOPING OTHERS SCORE [   ]

TABLE 4.4a   Management Competencies

Management Competencies (continued)

Planning

Develops and maintains a detailed master plan that
shows resource needs, budget, time schedules and
work to be done.   5 4 3 2 1

Assesses project design and implementation approach
often to assure that the project properly addresses the
business problem to be solved.   5 4 3 2 1

Ensures a common understanding and agreement
on the project scope and objectives and on any
subsequent changes   5 4 3 2 1

Maintains control of accepted changes to the project
plan and ensures that any changes are communicated
to all team members.   5 4 3 2 1

TOTAL PLANNING SCORE [   ]

Monitoring and Controlling

Regularly obtains status information from each project
team member on their assigned tasks, monitors
resource usage, schedule variances, and keeps the
project on schedule.   5 4 3 2 1

Identifies the economic and schedule consequences of
requested and/or mandated scope changes and
communicates these to management.   5 4 3 2 1

Accepts responsibility for resolving project issues,
especially scope changes, focusing on solutions,
recommendations, and actions.   5 4 3 2 1

Conducts a post-project review to identify what went
well, what should have been done differently and what
lessons were learned.   5 4 3 2 1

TOTAL MONITORING AND CONTROLLING SCORE [   ]

TABLE 4.4b   Management Competencies

Add the score value for each of the nineteen competency areas. The resulting scores are interpreted as follows:

Score Range	Project Manager Competency Level
4–7	Does not meet minimum competency level
8–10	Meets team leader minimum competency level
11–15	Meets project manager minimum competency level
16–18	Meets senior project manager minimum competency level
19–20	Meets program manager minimum competency level

Knowing your scores on each of the competencies will give you a rough guide as to where you should concentrate your development activities. You might want to ask your coworkers to assess your competencies and compare their responses with yours. You will discover that others do not perceive you as you perceive yourself. Their perceptions are reality regardless of how closely they agree with reality as you see it. Figure 4.2 is a typical competency assessment report*. The narrow filled rectangle is the individual's self-assessment; the filled square is the average assessment of the assessors; the unfilled rectangle is the inter-quartile range (the middle half of the data); and the end points of the solid line are the extreme observations that define the range of responses.

A Self-assessment

You have some decisions to make. And now is a good time to take stock of who you are and what you are really interested in doing. We have given you all of the data that is relevant to that decision. There

---

*Enterprise Information Insights, Inc., offers a web-enabled version of the Individual Competency Assessment. To get more information or to arrange to have an assessment conducted at your organization, contact them at 508-791-2062 or email them at rkw@eiicorp.com.

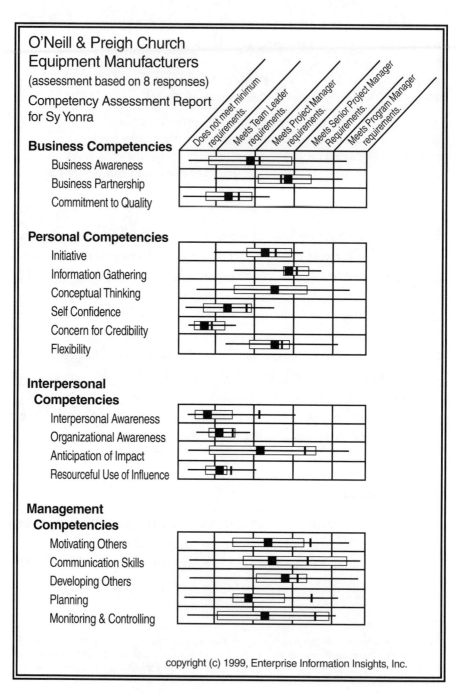

O'Neill & Preigh Church Equipment Manufacturers
(assessment based on 8 responses)
Competency Assessment Report for Sy Yonra

Does not meet minimum requirements.
Meets Team Leader requirements.
Meets Project Manager requirements.
Meets Senior Project Manager Requirements.
Meets Program Manager requirements.

Business Competencies
Business Awareness
Business Partnership
Commitment to Quality

Personal Competencies
Initiative
Information Gathering
Conceptual Thinking
Self Confidence
Concern for Credibility
Flexibility

Interpersonal Competencies
Interpersonal Awareness
Organizational Awareness
Anticipation of Impact
Resourceful Use of Influence

Management Competencies
Motivating Others
Communication Skills
Developing Others
Planning
Monitoring & Controlling

copyright (c) 1999, Enterprise Information Insights, Inc.

FIGURE 4.2 Competency Assessment Report

are two areas of importance that we suggest you assess: your environment and you.

Your External Environment

You have to supply the realities of the environment in which you work. For example, how supportive is the organization and your manager of your development? How important is it to them? What help do they provide? To what extent are development opportunities there for you to take advantage of?

Your Internal Environment

Let's assume that you have found the environment to be supportive and conducive to your professional development. The next area of concern is you personally. How excited are you about being a project manager now that you know "the good, the bad, and the ugly" about project management? Your successful development as a project manager is totally a function of what you are willing to put into the effort. No one is going to push you. No one (except,

> **A career path. . . is a look ahead at a planned course of growth and development of you as a professional.**

perhaps, your mentor and a few enlightened managers) is really interested in your future. In the final analysis, it's up to you.

A First Look at Your Career Path

A career path can be looked at in two ways. On the one hand it is a historical account of your professional life. On the other hand—and the one we focus on in this book—it is a look ahead at a planned course of growth and development of you as a professional. The first is a record of the past, and the second is a plan for the future.

Take a look at desirable futures.

What It Means to Have a Career Path

To have a career path simply means that you have taken a look at desirable futures and chosen the one that makes the most sense right now given where you are today.

> **To have a career path simply means that you have taken a look at desirable futures and have chosen the one that makes the most sense right now given where you are today.**

That career path will be dotted with several intermediate career goals that you will achieve along the way and culminating in a final career goal. Tomorrow you will be smarter than you are today, and those desirable futures will very likely change.

That's okay. It's part of the process. The important thing is that you have defined a future and you are taking meaningful and deliberate steps toward that future.

Career Paths Are Dynamic

We live and work in dynamic and changing times and we should expect our career paths to be dynamic and changing as well. Every new experience builds on its predecessor experiences and gives us new insights into the future. Opportunities arise and cause career interests to change (either temporarily or permanently), and hence career paths to change. Expect intermediate career goals to change frequently in response to opportunities arising at unexpected times.

Summary

You now have a complete picture of the project manager. You know what is done in each type of project manager role. You know what kinds of projects are managed as a project manager grows professionally. You know what competencies and skills they must possess to be successful at each stage of their professional development, and you have evaluated yourself against those standards. You have also taken a first look at what it means to have a career path. Let's move on to Chapter Five and complete your assessment of who you are.

chapter 5

Who Am I?

Introduction

No doubt everyone has heard about the temple in Greece that has the words "know thyself" over the entrance. How can you decide what kind of project manager you want to be unless you know what kind of person you are? Are you, for example, the kind of person who loves to do detailed planning? Do you like dealing with people? Do you love developing strategies and then trying to see them through to completion? These are important questions that must certainly be answered if you are to have confidence that project management is the right career for you. The purpose of this chapter is to introduce you to some resources that are available to help you with this self-assessment. In Chapter Eight we'll help you figure out how to get there (your career path).

This chapter is long and is packed with a number of commercially available assessment tools that you can opt to use to help better understand yourself with respect to your aptitude and readiness to be a project manager. We will explain each of them for you.

We start out with the most obvious—skill self-assessment. We identify fifty-four skills that you will need at some point in your project management career. At each stage of your career you will need to have a certain level of proficiency in many of these skills. The metric we use to measure proficiency is called Bloom's Taxonomy of Educational Objectives—Cognitive Domain. Though you might be totally unfamiliar with it, it has been used in adult education for over forty years and is easily understood and remembered. We will teach it to you and then have you self-assess your skills to be a project manager, using Appendix B. For those who want to know how they "stack up," we have included several figures (Figures 5.2–5.6) in this chapter that you can use to compare your profile against that of each of the four types of project manager that we discussed in Chapter Four.

As a transition to the other assessment tools, we introduce four general skill areas for your consideration: problem solving, conflict management and resolution, creative thinking, and decision making. Aspects of these four areas will have been measured in your skill self-assessment, but because they are so important to your success as a project manager, we want you to be aware of other tools for assessing them. These tools are discussed in the remainder of this chapter. Perhaps you are already familiar with some of them and have access to your results from having completed them at some earlier time. If so, great! That will give you even more benefits from this chapter. These tools are:

- Learning Styles Inventory
- Strength Deployment Inventory
- Myers-Briggs Personality Type Indicator
- Herrmann Brain Dominance Instrument
- Kirton Innovation-Adaptive Profile
- Strong Campbell Interest Inventory
- Self-analysis Process

You may wish to use some of these tools for your own personal edification. There is enough information presented in this chapter for you to follow up with any tool you are interested in. After a brief introduction to each of these seven assessment tools we will relate them to the practice of project management.

A word of caution as you approach this chapter is in order. There is clearly more information here than you could ever absorb, or even want to absorb, in one reading. For that reason we suggest that you quickly scan each of these seven tools in the first reading. Note the tools that are of particular interest or that you believe may be of value to you. You can return to them at some later time for a more in-depth reading.

Skill Profile of the World Class Project Manager

In 1990, Bob Wysocki set out to determine what it takes to be a world class project manager. He found that the characteristics of a world class project manager can be described by a set of fifty-four skills grouped into five general categories. Figure 5.1 lists those skills by general category.

Project Manager Skill Profile

Project Management Skills
Charter Development
Complexity Assessment
Cost Estimating
Cost Management
Critical Path Management
Detailed Estimating
Project Planning
Project Closeout
Project Management Software
Project Notebook Construction
Maintenance
Project Organization
Project Progress Assessment
Resource Acquisition
Resource Leveling
Resource Requirements
Schedule Development
Scope Management
Size Estimating

Management Skills
Delegation
Leadership
Managing Change
Managing Multiple Priorities
Meeting Management
Performance Management
Quality Management
Staff and Career Development
Staffing, Hiring, Selection

Business Skills
Budgeting
Business Assessment
Business Case Justification
Business Functions
Business Process Design
Company Products/Services
Core Applications System
Customer Service
Implementation
Planning: Strategic/Tactical
Product/Vendor Evaluation
Procedures and Policies
Systems Integration
Testing

Interpersonal Skills
Conflict Management
Flexibility
Influencing
Interpersonal Relations
Negotiating
Relationship Management
Team Management/Building

Personal Skills
Creativity
Decision Making/Critical Thinking
Presentations
Problem Solving/Trouble Shooting
Verbal Communications
Written Communications

FIGURE 5.1   Project Manager Skill Profile

The next thing we need is a metric to measure your level of proficiency in each skill. The metric will have to be applied uniformly across all skills and be easy to remember and apply. Rather than create our own, we have chosen to use a well-established metric that is very familiar to those in the adult education and skill assessment business: Bloom's Taxonomy of Educational Objectives—Cognitive Domain to measure skill levels. Bloom's Taxonomy has six levels that measure cognitive abilities, which are described as follows. It is based on observable and verifiable events as they relate to each of the skills. A definition of each of the six levels is as follows.

1.0 Knowledge (I can define the skill.)

Knowledge, as defined here, involves *the remembering or recalling* of ideas, materials, or phenomena. For measurement purposes, the recalled situations involve little more than bringing to mind the appropriate material. Although some alteration of the material may be required, this is a relatively minor part of the task.

2.0 Comprehension (I can explain how the skill is used.)

Comprehension involves those objectives, behaviors, or responses that represent an understanding of the literal message contained in a communication. In reaching such understanding, the individual may change the communication in his mind or in his overt responses to some parallel form more meaningful to him. He may also have responses that represent simple extensions beyond what is given in the communication itself.

3.0 Application (I have limited experience using the skill in simple situations.)

This skill level involves the use of abstractions in specific and concrete situations. The abstractions may be in the form of general ideas, rules, procedures, or generalized methods. The abstractions may also be technical principles, ideas, and theories that must be remembered and applied.

A demonstration of application is that the individual will use an abstraction correctly, given an appropriate situation in which no mode of solution is specified. The individual has the ability to apply generalizations and conclusions to real-life problems, and the ability to apply science principles, postulates, theorems, or other abstractions to new situations.

4.0 Analysis (I have extensive experience using the skill in complex situations.)

Analysis refers to the breakdown of a communication into its constituent elements or parts such that the relative hierarchy of ideas is made clear and/or the relationships between the ideas expressed are made explicit. Such analyses are intended to clarify the communication and to indicate how the communication is organized and the way in which it manages to convey its effects, as well as its basis and arrangement. Analysis deals with both the content and form of material.

5.0 Synthesis (I can adapt the skill to other uses.)

Synthesis means putting together elements and parts so as to form a whole. This involves the process of working with pieces, parts, elements, and so forth, and arranging and combining them in such a way as to constitute a pattern or structure not clearly there before.

6.0 Evaluation (I am recognized as an expert in using the skill by my peers.)

Evaluation involves making judgments about the value of material and methods for given purposes. Quantitative and qualitative judgments pertain to the extent to which material and methods satisfy criteria.

The criteria for evaluation may be those determined by the individual or those that are given to him.

Self-Assessment

So that you can assess yourself against the list of fifty-four skills, we have included an assessment questionnaire in Appendix B. It is formatted so that you can assess your own skills and profile yourself with respect to the four classes of project manager that we have defined. Answer the questionnaire now, before you continue with this chapter.

We're glad you are back, so let's move on. Now that you have assessed your proficiency with respect to each of the fifty-four skills, it is time to compare your profile with that of each of the four types of project managers. By doing so, you can determine your readiness to take on the responsibility of each project manager type. Figures 5.2 through 5.6 give the proficiency levels for these types of skills as a function of project manager class: project management, management, business, personal, and interpersonal. Recall from Chapter Four that the four project types and their associated project manager types are defined as follows:

- Type IV—Simple Projects. Led by a team leader.
- Type III—Organizationally Complex Projects. Led by a project manager or senior project manager.
- Type II—Technically Complex Projects. Led by a project manager or senior project manager.
- Type I—Critical Mission Projects. Led by a senior project manager or program manager.

As you examine Figures 5.2 through 5.6, note how the minimum proficiency levels in each of the skills change as you move from Type IV to Type I projects. By comparing your skill profile with these profiles, you can identify skills development needs as you progress through the ranks of project management.*

Expect to find several areas of deficiency. These will be skills to further develop and should appear in your tactical plans. See Chapter Eight for details on preparing your Professional Development Plan.

Project Manager Skill Assessment

If you think the block-and-tackle skills of project management are all it takes to be a successful project manager, read on. We have some news for you. Yes, it is true that you will need skills that relate directly to scoping, project planning, execution, tracking, and status reporting, as well as closing, but you need a lot more. To get our discussion started, let's examine four of the most obvious ones.

Problem Solving

We have practiced project management for over thirty-five years and have yet to be involved with a project that went according to plan. Something has always happened that sent us back to the drawing board scratching our heads and looking for a way out of the dilemma. The project manager needs to be able to assess the situation and find an acceptable answer. That will call upon her data-gathering skills, formulation of alternative solutions, ranking of alternatives, picking the best approach,

> **We have practiced project management for over thirty-five years and have yet to be involved with a project that went according to plan.**

---

* Enterprise Information Insights, Inc., offers a web-enabled service to assess skills and skill gaps of individuals and groups using self-assessments and user-defined 360-degree assessments. For more information or to arrange to have a skill assessment for your staff, contact us at 508-791-2062 or email us at rkw@eiicorp.com.

PROJECT MANAGEMENT SKILLS	IV	III	II	I
Charter Development	3	4	4	4
Complexity Assessment	-	3	3	4
Cost Estimating	3	4	4	5
Cost Management	3	4	4	5
Critical Path Management	3	4	4	4
Detailed Estimating	3	4	4	5
Project Planning (WBS, network, PERT, etc.)	3	4	4	4
Project Closeout	3	4	4	5
Project Management Software Expertise	3	4	4	4
Project Notebook Construction & Maintenance	3	4	4	4
Project Organization	-	3	3	5
Project Progress Assessment	2	3	3	4
Resource Acquisition	2	4	4	5
Resource Levelling	2	4	4	5
Resource Requirements	2	4	4	5
Schedule Development	3	3	3	4
Scope Management	3	4	4	5
Size Estimating	3	4	4	5
copyright (c) 1999, Enterprise Information Insights, Inc.				

FIGURE 5.2   Project Management Skills

MANAGEMENT SKILLS	IV	III	II	I
Delegation	3	4	4	5
Leadership	3	4	4	5
Managing Change	-	4	4	4
Managing Multiple Priorities	3	4	4	5
Meeting Management	3	4	4	5
Performance Management	-	3	3	4
Quality Management	3	3	3	4
Staff and Career Development	-	-	-	4
Staffing, Hiring, Selection	-	4	4	4

FIGURE 5.3   Management Skills

BUSINESS SKILLS	IV	III	II	I
Budgeting	-	3	3	4
Business Assessment	-	4	4	4
Business Case Justification	-	-	-	4
Business Functions	3	3	3	4
Business Process Design	-	3	3	3
Company Products/Services	-	3	3	3
Core Application Systems	3	3	3	3
Customer Service	-	-	-	3
Implementation	4	5	5	5
Planning: Strategic and Tactical	-	3	3	3
Product/Vendor Evaluation	-	-	-	4
Standards, Procedures, Policies	3	4	4	4
Systems and Technology Integration	-	4	4	4
Testing	4	4	4	4

FIGURE 5.4   Business Skills

INTERPERSONAL SKILLS	IV	III	II	I
Conflict Management	3	4	4	4
Flexibility	3	4	4	4
Influencing	-	3	3	4
Interpersonal Relations	3	4	4	4
Negotiating	-	3	3	4
Relationship Management	-	4	4	5
Team Management/Building	3	4	4	4

FIGURE 5.5 Interpersonal Skills

PERSONAL SKILLS	IV	III	II	I
Creativity	3	4	4	5
Decision Making/Critical Thinking	-	4	4	5
Presentations	-	4	4	4
Problem Solving/Trouble Shooting	4	4	4	5
Verbal Communications	3	4	4	4
Written Communications	3	3	3	4

copyright (c) 1999, Enterprise Information Insights, Inc.

FIGURE 5.6 Personal Skills

selling stakeholders on the best approach, implementing the chosen solution, and following up to make sure the problem was in fact solved.

The American educational system tends to create in students a bias to be solution-minded. There is a great deal of problem solving done throughout a person's school years, but most of it deals with structured problems that are called closed-ended—problems that have single answers. Examples include math or physics problems; or troubleshooting problems, in which something that once worked is now broken, and the troubleshooter has to find out what broke so that it can be repaired.

An entirely different category of problems, which are called open-ended, exists in which there is no single solution. Examples include how to design something, how to develop strategy for a project, and so on. There are many equally effective solutions to some of these problems. Furthermore, you find as you look around that *most* of the problems we encounter are open-ended, but our schooling has created in us a bias to look for single solutions, and this sometimes paralyzes us when we are dealing with open-ended situations. Or else we come up with a "quick fix" that does little more than eliminate a symptom of the problem momentarily but does not really address the problem itself.

We have found that projects typically fail at the very beginning because people on the team do not correctly define the problem to be solved by the project. So we consider this skill vital to your success as a project manager, and recommend that you set for yourself a goal to develop it. If you want an overview of how to solve both closed-ended and open-ended problems, you may want to consult the book *The Project Manager's Desk Reference* (Second Edition), by Jim Lewis (© 2000).

Conflict Management and Resolution

For some, this may be strange turf, but it is as important to the success of a project as any other skill—perhaps more so. This is because conflict is almost inevitable on any team. People differ in their ideas about how things should be done; they have conflicting personal objectives; and they have personalities that sometimes clash. So a project manager must know how to manage and resolve conflict.

Conflict management is important because conflict over ideas is a necessary part of the creative process in a project. But differing positions lead to interpersonal conflict because individuals identify with their ideas. So if one person says, "That's a stupid idea," you can expect that the person who thought of the idea will feel personally attacked, and this will lead to interpersonal conflict between the two individuals. For this reason, members of the team must be taught to critique ideas on their merits, saying something like, "The concern I have about this approach is that it does not address one aspect of the problem." This evaluates the idea without attacking the intelligence of the person who offered the suggestion.

> **Conflict management is important because conflict over ideas is a necessary part of the creative process in a project.**

Conflict management is thus the skill of drawing out all the ideas team members have on how to solve a problem, without letting them get into interpersonal conflict. Still, it seems inevitable that interpersonal conflicts will arise occasionally, and then the project manager must be able to engage in conflict resolution.

Fortunately, skill at both conflict management and conflict resolution can be acquired. Not everyone is equally good at it, any more than we are all good at any skill, but each of us can develop some level of competence if we want to. The key is to recognize that conflict often does not resolve itself. To think otherwise is a trap into which some project managers fall. These managers find dealing with conflict unpleasant; they don't like emotional behavior within their teams; and they hope that the conflict will just go away.

This is the "ostrich" response. Hiding your head in the sand will not make the problem disappear; in fact, it will usually make it get worse. So avoiding conflict is not the answer. If you give the individuals a reasonable amount of time to settle their differences and yet they make no headway, you are going to have to intervene.

This is one of those areas that many project managers dislike. You will see in the section of this chapter that covers thinking styles that individuals differ in their preference for dealing with "people problems," and many technologists and scientists have a low level of preference in this area, so they may avoid the situation altogether, or find it very noxious when they must intervene. As we have

> # Remember: Projects are people— not equipment, materials, or PERT diagrams.

counseled elsewhere in this book, if you absolutely detest dealing with people problems, then rethink your career. You don't want to be a project manager, because people issues come with the turf. Remember: Projects are people—not equipment, materials, or PERT diagrams.

Creative Thinking

Sometimes you might feel like the person in Vermont giving driving instructions: "You can't get there from here." If you are a strong process-oriented person, you may not be a good creative person. In this area it is especially important to draw upon the resources of your team members. Think outside the box. Don't be shackled by conventional thinking and practice. If you are ever going to be different, this is the time.

You will find (later in this chapter) that some individuals are naturally creative thinkers, and some are more analytical or detailed thinkers. However, it turns out that it is easier to help analytical thinkers learn to do creative thinking than vice versa. In fact, there are numerous books on this subject, and while it would be impossible to list all of them, a few we have found particularly useful are Michael Michalko's *Thinkertoys* (© 1991), Edward De Bono's *Serious Creativity* (© 1992), and Roger Von Oech's *A Whack on the Side of the Head* (© 1983).

Decision Making

How are you at defining the problem; gathering the necessary supporting data; formulating alternative solutions; and evaluating alternatives, picking the best one, and implementing it? A range of skills is required of the good decision maker. Many technical people will have some but not all of the requisite skills. If you don't possess them, it would be wise to make sure that your team collectively does.

Other Assessment Instruments

As we said earlier, problem solving, conflict management, creative thinking, and decision making are so important that we felt it necessary to identify a number of other assessment and diagnostic tools that you might want to use for these four skill areas. There are a number of commercially available assessment tools for individuals as well as for teams. The seven that are described here are ones we have used successfully in our consulting engagements for a number of years. We have chosen to include them in this book because we can speak from our own experiences in using them.

You will be familiar with some of them. For those you are familiar with, you might want to refer to those sections and read how the scores and results from these instruments relate to your readiness and adaptability to project management. If you have no familiarity with any of them, this is a good time to become so. You might want to look further into a few of them and consider assessing yourself against them.

Use this section as a reference for later development planning. This first reading is one that you should do quickly just to create familiarity with each instrument. You can return to this section later, when more details are needed or as you decide which instruments will be useful to you and which you will assess yourself against.

The Learning Styles Inventory

The Learning Styles Inventory (LSI) was originally developed by David Kolb in 1981 and is marketed through the Hay McBer Training Resources Group. The LSI consists of twelve questions that are designed to help you evaluate the way you learn. Although you may already know that you prefer to experiment with something new rather than have someone lecture you on its use, the LSI will help you under-

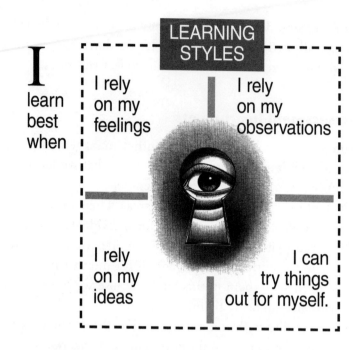

stand exactly how you learn and what you might do to improve your learning abilities. The questions ask you to rank your preferences for four different choices in several different learning situations. For example, one of the questions asks:

Your response is to rank the four choices from most like you (a 4 ranking) to least like you (a 1 ranking). The inventory is self-administered and self-scored. Following an algorithm that is explained in the inventory, the rankings are tabulated and presented in four dimensions: abstract conceptualization, active experimentation, concrete experience, and reflective observation.

A simple example will help clarify these four dimensions. Let's assume you want to learn to swim. If you say, "I'd like to read about the principles of buoyancy in a liquid medium," that is an example of abstract conceptualization. If you say, "I'd like to get in the pool, but I want someone next to me in the event I start to sink," that is active ex-

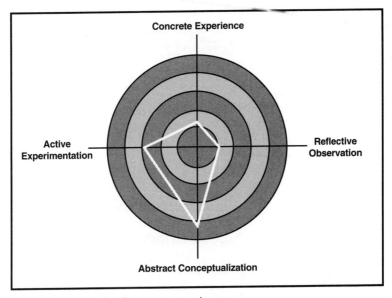

FIGURE 5.7 Example of a Learning Styles Inventory

perimentation. If you say, "Throw me in the pool and I will figure it out on the way down," that is concrete experience. And finally, if you say, "Can't I just watch for a while and see how it is done?" that is reflective observation. All four are valid modes of learning and all four are used to some extent by every one of us. We just happen to prefer one over the other in certain situations. Figure 5.7 illustrates a typical result from an individual who strongly favors abstract conceptualization and active experimentation over concrete experience and reflective observation. Individuals who are characterized by this kite configuration (that's what the data display is called) are good problem solvers and are results-oriented. These types of individuals generally are found in the more technical or specialist careers, such as that of project managers.

These four dimensions can be further mapped into a two-dimensional graphic, as shown in Figure 5.8. The data point is the result of mapping the kite from Figure 5.7 into these two dimensions.

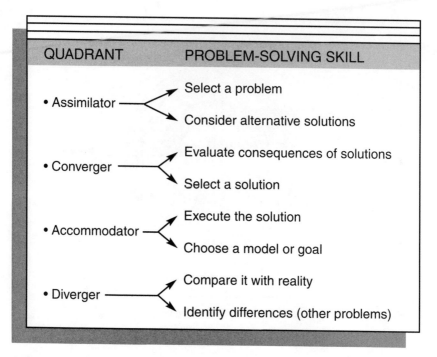

FIGURE 5.8 The Learning Style Types

The horizontal dimension is the difference between the scores on active experimentation and reflective observation. The vertical dimension is the difference between the scores on abstract conceptualization and concrete experience. The Learning Styles Inventory booklet gives you the formulae for making these calculations. By presenting the data in this format, you can compare your learning styles to that of the problem-solving process. As shown below, each quadrant has a particular strength when it comes to problem solving. Because of the close association between problem solving and decision making, this approach works equally well there.

It would be unusual for you to be strong in all four quadrants, but at least the data will tell you where your strengths and weaknesses lie. Then you will be prepared to do something about it. Namely, play to your strengths for now, and take steps to correct your weaknesses in the future. What quadrant are you strong in? Does this correlate with how you perceive yourself? Most people agree that it does.

The Strength Deployment Inventory

The Strength Deployment Inventory (SDI) was developed by Elias Porter in 1973. It consists of ten questions that ask about your behavior when everything is going well, and ten questions that ask about your behavior when everything is going wrong. Here is one question from the first ten:

I find those relationships most gratifying in which I can be . . .

_____ of support to a strong leader in whom I have faith.

_____ the one who provides the leadership others want to follow.

_____ neither a leader nor a follower but free to pursue my own independent way.

Now here is a question from the next ten:

When another person insists on having his or her own way, I tend to . . .

_____ put my wishes aside for the time being and go along with that person.

_____ put up counterarguments and try to get the person to change.

_____ respect the person's right to follow his or her interest as long as there is no interference with mine.

You will answer by distributing ten points across the three responses. The more points you allocate to a response, the more it reflects your behavior. There are no right or wrong answers. The instrument is simply describing behavior.

One of the strengths of the SDI is that it is self-scoring and self-analyzing. You don't need a high-priced consultant to tell you what the data is saying. The SDI booklet contains, in addition to the twenty questions, all of the instructions and data templates you will need to do a complete analysis of the question responses.

Figure 5.9 is the plot of the data from associates we know. The base of the arrow describes behavior when things are going fine. The arrowhead describes behavior when things are going wrong. We can learn quite a bit about how a person deals with conflict from an analysis of the arrows. First, note that person A is described by an arrow that lies nearly inside the circle (aka, hub) in the middle of the diagram. That person does not display any strong tendencies to one form of behavior over another whether in conflict or not. They are very difficult to read. You can't tell whether they are in a conflict mode of behavior or not. That can be both a strength and a weakness. It is a strength in the sense that this individual weighs input and opinions from all concerned before making any decision. It is a weakness in that the lack of decisiveness may be perceived as a wishy-washy or unstable person. In fact, the person is very much influenced by the situation and may behave quite differently from one situation to the next. He or she may tend to be very deliberate and not prone to knee-jerk reactions and decisions. If you have concluded that this type of pattern is typical of good project managers, you are right. But that doesn't mean your arrow has to be in the hub in order for you to be a good project manager. Regardless of how the arrow is positioned, you can be a good project manager. It is just a fact that arrows distributed in or near the hub are indicative of good project managers.

Person B is quite different. He or she is very aggressive and results driven and, when placed in conflict, takes a very analytical point of view. This individual is very weak in people skills in both normal and conflict situations.

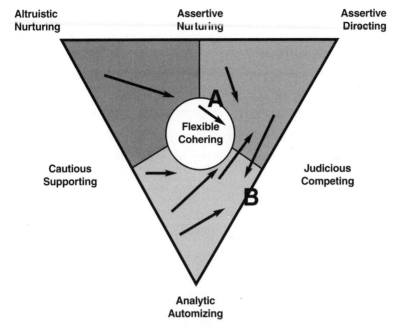

FIGURE 5.9   Examples of Strength Development Inventory Scores

The Myers-Briggs Personality Type Indicator

Perhaps a more accurate heading for this section would be "Who am I?" because it deals with the attributes of people as they relate to project management. We do not claim to have a complete answer to the question "What kind of person makes a good project manager?" Nor do we have a test that you can administer to determine such a thing.

What we do offer are some insights to such issues as personality, thinking styles, and other attributes that affect one's ability to be a project manager. We leave it to you as an individual to make your own decision about your temperament and the likelihood that project management is the proper career path for you.

Every year approximately 1 million individuals take the Myers-Briggs Personality Type Indicator (MBTI) to assess their personalities. The model was based on Swiss psychiatrist Carl Jung's theories of personalities, and the instrument was developed by Isabel Myers-Briggs. It measures an individual's preference for interacting with the world on four dimensions. These are discussed in the text that follows. Each dimension is designated by two letters, as shown in parenthesis beside the heading for the section.

Extroversion-Introversion (E/I). Jung postulated that we have two ways of becoming energized. The person who is introverted draws energy from within. Ideas, concepts, and dreams fuel the introverted individual. The extrovert, on the other hand, is energized by things outside—people, places, things, and conditions. Contrary to popular misconception, introverts are not hermits! They can interact freely and comfortably with other human beings; it's just that they get most excited and stimulated by their internal world of thoughts and ideas.

In the same way, extroverts are not "party animals" all the time. They also have their quiet moments. But they do gain energy from interacting with other people, whereas an introvert may feel a bit drained by long interaction. In fact, introverts need time every day to "recharge their batteries," by being alone with their thoughts, whereas the extrovert, if left alone for too long, begins to feel deprived of the external sensory stimulation on which they thrive.

Interestingly, because extroverts draw so much energy from interacting with others, they often do not understand the need of the introvert to be alone. They think this is abnormal, and do sometimes see them as hermits, because they don't understand that everyone is not energized in the same way.

Approximately 75 percent of the American population is extroverted, and 25 percent is introverted. In technical groups, however, this statistic tends to

> **Approximately 75 percent of the American population is extroverted, and 25 percent is introverted. In technical groups, however, this statistic tends to be reversed . . .**

be reversed, with 75 percent of engineers, programmers, and scientists being introverts.

What does this mean? For one thing, it has a lot to do with how they thrive in the work environment. Introverts are more distracted by environmental noise than are extroverts. They cannot think in a noisy workplace. So where do we put engineers and programmers? In bull pens and cubicles, where they are constantly being thrown off track in their work by all the noises around them.

Meanwhile, the extrovert is happily chugging away at his work with the radio blaring, tapping his foot to the music, or humming along, totally oblivious to the fact that his radio is driving his introverted cube mate to distraction and causing her to have thoughts of assassinating her noisy associate.

From a productivity point of view, organizations treat their human resources worse than their capital equipment. There is a large machine shop in the southeast that has almost all computer-controlled machines. If these are not air-conditioned, the computer controls will quit. So the shop is comfortable even when it is 100 degrees outside.

Yet we put people who are paid to think in an environment that makes it impossible for them to do so, and then wonder why they are so unproductive! Go figure.

On the introversion-extroversion scale, you get a score for each, rather than a single score that says you are somewhere on a single dimension. So you can have eighteen points for introversion, and twenty-six points for extroversion, because we all have some tendency to go in both directions. Naturally, you can blow either scale off the map, having zero points on one and all of your points on the other.

Which is best? Individuals who have zero points on one and all of their points on the other dimension may actually be a bit compulsive about their preference—that is, if they are strongly extroverted, they find aloneness to be almost unbearable. If they are introverted, they find heavy doses of interaction with others to be painful. For that reason, it is probably a little better to have some points on both scales, but if you don't, it doesn't mean you should be concerned about it, either. The instrument measures your *preference* for certain modes, and you can go with or against those preferences. The choice is yours.

Sensing and Intuition (S/N). The next scale measured by the MBTI is sensing and intuition. Note that the letter "N" is used for intuition, as we have already used "I" for introversion. This scale describes the ways in which you perceive or acquire information. It's how you go about finding out about things.

> **This scale describes the ways in which you perceive or acquire information.**

If you prefer sensing to gather information, you use your five physical senses. Like Columbo, the detective, sensors may be inclined to say, "Just the facts, ma'am, just the facts." They rely on what is given in the here and now, and are realistic and practical. They are usually good at remembering and working with facts.

Intuition is preferred by some to gather information. Using intuition, they sense meanings, relationships, and possibilities that go beyond the information presented by the senses. Through intuition, they see the big picture and try to understand the essential pattern of the situation. They become good at seeing new possibilities and new ways of doing things. They value imagination and inspiration.

Thinking and Feeling (T/F).   This scale looks at how you make decisions. Once you have acquired information through sensing or intuition, you need to do something with that information. You may reach conclusions, make decisions, or form opinions.

For those who prefer thinking, they decide objectively. They look at the logical consequences of their choices and make decisions by weighing the pros and cons. They look for objective truth, as opposed to subjective opinions.

Those who go on feeling, on the other hand, consider what is important to you or to others and decide on the basis of values. There is no requirement that logic be involved. If you are making a

> **For those who prefer thinking, they decide objectively. . . . Those who go on feeling, on the other hand, consider what is important to you or to others and decide on the basis of values.**

decision for yourself, you ask how much you care, or how much personal investment you have in the issue. Note that "feeling" means making decisions based on values rather than facts—it does *not* refer to emotion.

Judging and Perceiving (J/P).   This scale describes how you orient yourself in relation to the outside world. This scale refers back to the previous two. If you take a judging position toward the world, you primarily adopt thinking or feeling as your approach, whereas if you take a perceiving position, then you adopt sensing or intuition.

Those who adopt a judging attitude (thinking or feeling) tend to live in a planned, orderly way. Such individuals want to regulate their life and control it. You make decisions, come to closure, and then carry on. People who have a preference for judging like for things to be structured and organized and like to tidy up loose ends. Unfortunately the word "judging" has a negative connotation, but it should not be interpreted that way. Any of the types can be judgmental.

> **Those who adopt a judging attitude (thinking or feeling) tend to live in a planned, orderly way. . . . Perceiving individuals like to live flexible, spontaneous lives.**

Perceiving individuals like to live flexible, spontaneous lives. They do not like structure, are not fond of orderly routine, but prefer to keep their options open. They prefer to understand life rather than control it. They stay open to experience, and like to adapt to the moment.

Personality Types.   One letter from each scale is used to define a personality type. For example, we have ESTJ, ESTP, INFP, ISFJ, and so on, to get sixteen different types. Each will have slightly different attributes based on the specific combination of preferences. Naturally, since most people have some preference for both dimensions on a scale, you have a lot more than sixteen possibilities. In fact, the nuances of personality are almost unlimited, as you would expect for human beings. We are just too complex to be able to precisely "pigeonhole" into a single category in which we can say, "That's you!" However, of the million individuals who take the MBTI each year, the vast majority of them agree that there is an uncanny resemblance of their personality type to their true self. They may say, "That's pretty much me." We say then, that the MBTI has "face validity." This means that it appears to measure what it is supposed to measure.

Temperaments. One problem with the sixteen types is that there are too many of them to keep up with in your head. Furthermore, it seems that individuals who like to observe people have known for centuries that there are four temperaments that describe people in a rather broad-stroke manner. David Keirsey has written extensively on temperaments in his book, *Please Understand Me II.*

Temperaments make use of only two letters of the sixteen to designate personality. These two-letter combinations are based on two dimensions of behavior that are diagrammed in Figure 5.10 on the following page. One dimension is that of communication, whether one uses words in an abstract or a concrete way. The other is that of the cooperative or utilitarian use of tools. The word "tools" is a term that Keirsey uses in a very broad sense—a tool can be anything from an actual tool like a screwdriver to an automobile or computer.

Notice that intuitive individuals tend to use words abstractly, while sensing individuals tend to use them more concretely. For tools, we see that feeling and judging individuals use them cooperatively, while thinking and perceiving individuals use them in a utilitarian way.

By abstract communication, Keirsey means that a person talks in figurative, symbolic, general terms, compared to literal, specific, and factual ways for the concrete communicator. He suggests that abstract communication is more symbolic, in which the person tries to bring to mind something that can't be seen immediately, whereas the concrete communicator sends signals—messages that point to something that can be seen.

In terms of tool use, Keirsey says that the cooperative use of tools means a person would use a tool in a way that has been approved by others. Utilitarian use means that the person would use a tool however it works, regardless of whether that way has been approved by others. To quote Keirsey, "Cooperators try to get where they want to go by getting along with others. . . . Utilitarians tend to go after what they want in the most effective ways possible . . . " (Keirsey, © 1998, pg. 28).

	Words	
	Abstract	**Concrete**
Cooperative	Idealists **NF** 10% of population	Guardians **SJ** 45% of population
Utilitarian	Rationals **NT** 5% of population	Artisans **SP** 40% of population

(Tools)

FIGURE 5.10 The Kiersey Temperaments

Intellect

Keirsey contends that we have varying abilities to use diplomatic, strategic, logistical, or tactical skills, with each of the temperaments being better at one of these than the other three. This has definite implications for project managers, as we shall see.

"Diplomacy is the ability to deal with people in a skillful, tactful manner . . . " (Keirsey, © 1998, pg. 123). Tactical skill means ". . . the art of making moves to better one's position in the here and now . . . " (Keirsey, © 1998, pg. 38). "Logistics is the procurement, distribution, service, and replacement of material goods" (Keirsey, © 1998, pg. 82). And finally, "Strategy has to do with identifying the ways and means necessary and sufficient to achieve a well-defined goal" (Keirsey, © 1998, pg. 169).

> **Notice that intuitive individuals tend to use words abstractly, while sensing individuals tend to use them more concretely.**

Organizations
sometimes treat
their human
resources worse
than their capital
equipment.

In describing the four temperaments as follows, we will see how these skills come into play for each temperament, and how they may affect the kind of project manager a person may be.

The NF/Idealist Temperament

The NF temperament is in the abstract-cooperative cell, and is called an idealist (Figure 5.11). Keirsey says that this temperament makes up about 10 percent of our population. A notable example from history is Mahatma Gandhi.

The idealist tends to excel at diplomatic skills.

The idealist tends to excel at diplomatic skills. Keirsey suggests that the rank order for the four kinds of intellect are as follows for idealists:

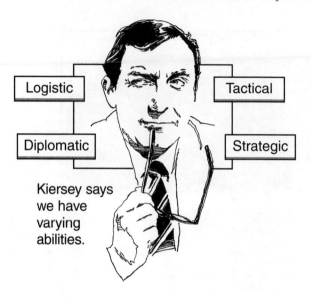

Logistic

Tactical

Diplomatic

Strategic

Kiersey says
we have
varying
abilities.

1. Diplomacy
2. Strategy
3. Logistics
4. Tactics

Thus, we would expect that the idealist project manager would excel at dealing with "people" issues, such as team building, politics, managing conflict, attending to the personal needs of team members, and so on. They would also be relatively good at seeing the "big picture" in a project, and in developing a good project strategy. On the other hand, the idealist would be less skilled at logistics, which would involve keeping the team supplied with things they need to do their jobs, and tactical issues, which would be involved in the detailed planning of execution steps in a project. These details would be better handled by other members of the team.

Idealists tend to be helpers. Depending on the specific four-letter type (whether ENFJ, INFJ, ENFP, or INFP), an idealist may be a

Words		
	Abstract	**Concrete**
Cooperative	Idealists **NF** 10% of population	Guardians **SJ** 45% of population
Utilitarian	Rationals **NT** 5% of population	Artisans **SP** 40% of population

(Tools — left axis label)

FIGURE 5.11 The Idealist Temperament

NF Diplomatic Roles	
Mentor	**Advocate**
ENFJ: Teacher	ENFP: Champion
INFJ: Counselor	INFP: Healer

FIGURE 5.12 NF Diplomatic Roles

mentor or an advocate for others. Figure 5.12 shows these various role variants. (See Keirsey, © 1998, pg. 126ff for more information.)

The SJ/Guardian Temperament

The SJ temperament is called a guardian, and is, like the idealist, co-operative in the use of tools (Figure 5.13). Unlike the idealist, however, the guardian uses words in a concrete manner, while the idealist is more abstract in communicating. The guardian is very concerned with security, control, factual information, compliance, conformity, obedience to rules, and so on. He or she works hard to "make and enforce the laws that govern action, insisting that only by establishing and obeying rules and regulations can we hope to maintain civil order, and thus safeguard our homes, communities, and businesses" (Keirsey, © 1998, pg. 80).

> **The guardian is very concerned with security, control, factual information, compliance, conformity, obedience to rules . . .**

The guardian is best at dealing with logistics of the four temperaments. The order of their skills, according to Keirsey, is

1. Logistics
2. Tactics
3. Diplomacy
4. Strategy

They will also be good at working out the tactics needed to make an overall strategy work, but may not be quite as good at dealing with people (diplomacy), or at developing the strategy itself.

Keirsey says that guardians and rationals make up nearly 80 percent of corporations, although the two groups combined constitute only about 50 percent of our total population. Furthermore, they are diagonally opposite each other in the matrix, which means that they have

		Words	
		Abstract	Concrete
Cooperative		Idealists **NF** 10% of population	Guardians **SJ** 45% of population
Utilitarian		Rationals **NT** 5% of population	Artisans **SP** 40% of population

FIGURE 5.13 The Guardian Temperament

maximum room for conflict. The guardian communicates concretely, while the rational talks abstractly, making it difficult for them to understand each other. Simultaneously, the guardian is cooperative in the use of tools, while the rational is utilitarian. The rational does whatever works, violating the "rules" of proper tool use if necessary, an act that is abhorrent to the rule-governed guardian and threatens the very fabric of social order (or so thinks the guardian).

Rationals are the natural strategists.

Since many engineers are rationals and many managers are guardians, you can see that these two groups tend to be at each other's throats fairly often. The engineer believes that his guardian manager has no clue what he is doing (which may well be true), doesn't value his work, and is too rigid. The guardian thinks the engineer is flaky, undisciplined, and has his head in the clouds. Only the idealist is more unrealistic, but at least the idealist is cooperative in the use of tools, while the rational is a rebel.

SJ Logistical Roles	
Administrator	**Conservator**
ESTJ: Supervisor	ESFJ: Provider
ISTJ: Inspector	ISFJ: Protector

FIGURE 5.14 SJ Logistical Roles

The logistical roles of the guardian are shown in Figure 5.14 (adapted from Keirsey, © 1998, pg. 84).

The NT/Rational Temperament

As we have just seen, the rational is opposite the guardian in terms of the dimensions of temperament, and is also the smallest temperament in our population, comprising only about 5 percent of it, according to Keirsey.

They are concerned with logic, and sometimes seem detached and distant to other people. They may be lacking in social skills, having spent much of their lives immersed in books and learning.

Rationals are the natural strategists. Strategy is defined as the way and means for achieving a goal. The rational will be good at developing a game plan for a project. Here is the order that Keirsey gives for the intellect of rationals (Keirsey, © 1998, pg. 172):

1. Strategy
2. Diplomacy
3. Tactics
4. Logistics

Notice that the order of these is exactly reversed for rationals and guardians. And, though they are opposites and tend to experience con-

		Words	
		Abstract	**Concrete**
Cooperative		Idealists **NF** 10% of population	Guardians **SJ** 45% of population
Utilitarian		Rationals **NT** 5% of population	Artisans **SP** 40% of population

FIGURE 5.15 The Rational Temperament

siderable conflict, a project team needs both to succeed. The rational will be good at strategy and diplomacy, but less skilled at tactics and logistics. They will be less inclined to focus on detailed project plans. Figure 5.16 shows the NT strategic roles (Keirsey, © 1998, pg. 173).

It is interesting to note that diplomacy is the second-highest intellect for the rational, since they are so often thought of as being socially maladjusted. And they may be, but only because of lack of practice at diplomatic skills. However, they have the *potential* to become skilled diplomats, which is much needed by project managers who have no authority and must use influence to get their jobs done.

The SP/Artisan Temperament

"Artisans tend to become masters in the making of solid, practical things" (Keirsey, © 1998, pg. 33). They may be the least-represented group in corporations, because they absolutely detest the rules and

NT Strategic Roles	
Coordinator	**Engineer**
ENTJ: Fieldmarshal	ENTP: Inventor
INTJ: Mastermind	INTP: Architect

FIGURE 5.16 The NT Strategic Roles

regulations handed down by guardian managers. Nor do they like the structure of daily routines. (See Figure 5.17.)

In schools, which are largely administered by guardian teachers and principals, and which cater to a guardian mentality, the artisan is bored to distraction. Artisan children are often labeled "hyperactive" since they can't sit still while subjects that they find boring are presented, and in the American drug-oriented culture, may have their behavior controlled by Ritalin. After all, their unwillingness to conform to rule-governed behavior prescribed by guardians is a threat to social order, and believing that control must be maintained, the guardian seeks to regain order by subduing the hapless artisan.

> **"Artisans tend to become masters in the making of solid, practical things."**

Keirsey suggests that the artisan is most talented at tactical skills. If the rational can suggest a strategy to be followed, the artisan can make that strategy work. The following is Keirsey's ranking of their intellectual skills:

1. Tactics
2. Logistics

		Words	
		Abstract	Concrete
Tools	Cooperative	Idealists **NF** 10% of population	Guardians **SJ** 45% of population
	Utilitarian	Rationals **NT** 5% of population	Artisans **SP** 40% of population

FIGURE 5.17 The Artisan Temperament

3. Strategy
4. Diplomacy

We could conclude that artisans would be excellent at working out the detailed schedule for a project (if you can find one in your organization). Note that artisans represent almost 40 percent of the population, but only perhaps 5 percent of the organizational population. And if an artisan does work in a company, he/she will probably be seen as unconventional, nonconformist, and a bit "wacky."

Figure 5.18 lists the artisan's tactical roles (Keirsey, © 1998, pg. 40).

This is of necessity a very abbreviated sketch of Myers-Briggs types and Keirsey temperaments. We hope the sketch will give you some idea of how your personality may affect the way in which you approach projects. As Ned Herrmann has suggested, we believe that any of the temperaments can be successful project managers, but each will approach the discipline in a different way. The NT rational will be

SP Tactical Roles	
Operator	**Entertainer**
ESTP: Promoter	ESFP: Performer
ISTP: Crafter	ISFP: Composer

FIGURE 5.18 The Artisan Tactical Roles

very keen on project strategy, the NF idealist on diplomatic relationships with all stakeholders, the SJ guardian on project logistics, and the SP artisan on project tactics. The important thing to note is that a team that lacks any of the temperaments will have to compensate by dealing with the area best handled by the missing temperament. Since all four have some of each of the intellectual skills, this is not an insurmountable obstacle, but awareness of the deficiency is important, or else the missing area may be neglected to the detriment of the project. If you want to learn more about this area, we suggest you consult the following: Keirsey, 1998 and Kroeger, 1988.

The Herrmann Brain Dominance Instrument (HBDI®)

This is a very powerful tool because it can be used to describe a project, to describe an individual team member, and to describe the entire team. We know of no other tool that has this breadth of application to project management. It was developed by Ned Herrmann, to whom we have dedicated this book. Ned developed the HBDI during his tenure as manager of management education at General Electric. The tool was first used in the late 1970s. Through a series of 120 questions, a person's thinking styles are mapped into the four-sided graphic shown in Figure 5.19.

Thinking Styles. When Ned became interested in the subject of thinking, brain research had suggested that people are either right-brained or left-brained in their preference. Those who prefer left-brained thinking would deal with logic, analysis, order, and so on, while the right-brained individuals would be more be more conceptual and less orderly in their thinking. As Ned studied the literature and tried to understand people in his training programs, he decided something was missing.

He eventually postulated that thinking was influenced by another dimension of the brain, which he surmised was the cerebral and limbic components of the brain. By adding this dimension, he could map thinking styles into the four quadrants of Figure 5.19.

Whether thinking preferences are actually determined by brain physiology remains open to question, but after thirty years of research, we believe that the folks at Herrmann International have demonstrated the validity of the four different thinking modes. At this time, more than 1 million individuals have taken the HBDI, and there are over 300,000 profiles stored in the Herrmann computer, representing almost every imaginable

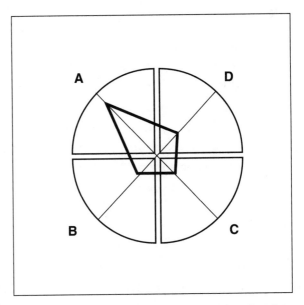

FIGURE 5.19   The Four-Quadrant Thinking Styles of the HBDI

job discipline and many different nationalities. So let's take a look at each of the quadrants and then see what they may tell us about project managers.

The A-Quadrant

The thinking associated with the A-Quadrant can be described as logical, analytical, technical, mathematical, and problem-solving (see Figure 5.19). People with a strong preference to think in these ways are also attracted to professions that require such thinking. Examples of such careers include technical, legal, and financial areas, including

> ... **The A-Quadrant can be described as logical, analytical, technical, mathematical, and problem-solving.**

accounting and tax law, engineering, mathematics, and some middle management positions.

A project manager with a single-dominant profile in the A-Quadrant could be expected to be very logical, to be interested in technical issues affecting the project, to be inclined to analyze status reports carefully, and to be keen on problem solving. If he/she has very little preference for thinking in the other quadrants (particularly the C-Quadrant), this person may be seen as cold, uncaring, and interested only in the problems presented by the project.

The B-Quadrant

The B-Quadrant is similar to the A-Quadrant, but with significant differences. Words that describe the B-Quadrant are organizational, administrative, conservative, controlled, and planning. This is the preferred thinking of many managers, administrators, and planners, bookkeepers, foremen, and manufacturers. Individuals who have single-dominant profiles in the B-Quadrant could be expected to be concerned with the detailed plans of a project, and with keeping everything organized and controlled. Note that individuals with financial interests who are dominant in the A-Quadrant will probably

be financial managers, whereas those with dominant B-Quadrant profiles may be drawn to cost accounting.

. . . B-Quadrant descriptors are organizational, administrative, conservative, controlled and planning.

If you want someone to pay attention to detail, to dot all the letter "i" and cross the letter "t", then you want someone who has a strong preference for this quadrant. If they have a single dominant profile, however, they may see the trees and be unaware of the forest.

The C-Quadrant

People with single-dominant profiles in the A- or B-Quadrants probably see individuals with strong C-Quadrant preferences as be-

ing very "touchy-feely." Words that describe this quadrant are interpersonal, emotional, musical, spiritual, and talkative. Individuals with single-dominant C profiles would be very "feeling" and people-oriented. Such individuals are often nurses, social workers, musicians, teachers, counselors, or ministers.

> **Words that describe the C-quadrant are interpersonal, emotional, musical, spiritual, and talkative.**

A project manager with a single-dominant C profile would naturally be concerned with the interpersonal aspects of the project, perhaps to the detriment of getting the work done. Such an individual would be drawn to the coordination of project activities with people both inside and outside the team, and

would be a relationship builder. For highly political projects, this would be a good bias to have, as long as other members of the team are attending to the work itself.

In fact, you will remember we have said several times that projects are people, and dealing with people is one aspect of project management that some individuals find distasteful. So you can expect that the people who have very low C-Quadrant scores on the HBDI will be bothered by this aspect of the job. Our counsel is that such people *can* develop this skill if they have the desire to, but given very low scores in the C-Quadrant naturally will mean this is not their "cup of tea." So they will have to work very hard at this aspect of the job if they want to manage projects.

There is an interesting finding about how we behave in terms of our least-preferred thinking styles. Jim Lewis has a very strong D-Quadrant preference, with B-Quadrant being his least preferred. This means he loves developing concepts, and dislikes doing detail work. However, if he must do detail work in order to ensure one of his ideas[1] seeing the light of day, he can become very motivated to do so. What this means, then, is that you can be motivated to deal with the "touchy-feely" stuff if it means achieving success in terms of your other thinking preferences. Take Bob Wysocki, who has a very strong A-Quadrant preference, with the C-Quadrant being his least preferred. Bob holds a PhD in mathematical statistics and has always viewed himself as a problem solver. His weak C-Quadrant score is testimony that he is musically challenged. His wife will testify to that fact as well.

The D-Quadrant

Words that describe this quadrant are artistic, holistic, imaginative, synthesizing, and conceptualizing. Individuals who have single-dominant D-Quadrant profiles are often drawn to careers that involve entrepreneurial effort, facilitation, advising, or consulting, being sales leaders and artists. These are the "idea" people on a team, and they enjoy synthesizing ideas from several sources to create something new from that combination.

This is the natural domain of people who are thought of as being creative. At the beginning of this chapter we discussed the need for creative thinking in projects. So you may conclude that if you are primarily a "left-brain" thinker, having strong preferences for A- or B-Quadrant thinking, and low preference for thinking in the D-Quadrant, then you are out of luck. Not so. It turns out that it is easier for left-brain thinkers to learn to do conceptual or creative thinking than it is for conceptual thinkers to do analytical or detail thinking.

> **Words that describe the D-quadrant are artistic, holistic, imaginative, synthesizing, and conceptualizing.**

Project managers who have single-dominant D-Quadrant profiles could be expected to be very "big picture" in their thinking. They may run the risk of seeing the forest without realizing that it consists of a

bunch of trees. They are generally good at thinking strategically, so in planning a project, the D-Quadrant thinker will develop a "game plan," but will need help from B-Quadrant thinkers to turn it into something practical.

Double, Triple, and Quadruple Profiles

In this book we have limited space to detail each instrument, so we will have to limit our discussion about various profiles. As you can imagine, you can have a wide variety of profiles. We have discussed single-dominant profiles and what they may mean for project managers. But suppose you have strength in two quadrants? Or three? Or all four? What would that mean? An example is shown in Figure 5.20 on page 127. This individual has a double-dominant profile, but interestingly, it is across the diagonal between Quadrants B and D. The person was an interior designer, and we asked her, "Do you sometimes talk yourself out of some good ideas?" She admitted that she did. The reason was that she would conceive of the idea by using

her D-Quadrant thinking, and then when she tried to work out the details of how to execute the idea, she would begin to find problems and throw it out.

On the positive side, though, she did have the desire to make her designs a reality, something that a person with a single dominant D-Quadrant profile may not otherwise do. The single-dominant person may conceive of all kinds of good ideas but not implement them.

Think of this person in a project manager's role. We would guess that she would be good at seeing the "big picture" of the project, and at developing project strategy, but she would also be interested in doing detailed implementation planning as well. In other words, she could see both the forest *and* the trees.

The Relationship Between the HBDI and Myers-Briggs. Ned Herrmann postulated that it is the brain that in some way influences a person's thinking preferences, so it may be informative to ask if the brain influences personality characteristics. Researchers have found that there is a correlation between the thinking-feeling scale of My-ers-Briggs and the HBDI. The thinking end of the scale correlates with the A-Quadrant, and the feeling end with the C-Quadrant. Also, the sensing-intuition scale correlates with the remaining quadrants. Sensing correlates with the B-Quadrant, and intuition with the D-Quadrant. This is shown in Figure 5.21 on page 128.

Work Motivation and the HBDI. One aspect of thinking preferences that you should consider is that you probably have a least-preferred thinking style (or several). Jim Lewis's is the B-Quadrant, which requires lots of attention to detail. He would find a project requiring such thinking to be drudgery. When he was an engineer, he disliked the detail work involved in reviewing drawings or making sure a bill of materials was exactly right. It was vital work, but he hated it. So knowing your most- and least-preferred thinking styles should help you determine when a particular kind of project is a good match for you, or what you should do when there is a mismatch.

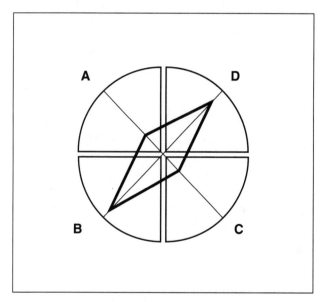

FIGURE 5.20 Interior Designer's Double Dominant Profile

Is There a Best Profile? Ned Herrmann was always careful to say that individuals with almost any profile *can* do most jobs. The HBDI measures one's *preference* for thinking, not one's *ability*. There is, of course, a relationship. When you have a strong preference for something, you tend to do it over and over, and in the process, become good at it. So we can expect that our profiles will bear some relationship to our skills, simply because we have practiced thinking in some quadrants more than in others, and have gotten good at those particular preferred modes.

Ned did postulate that there may be an ideal profile for a chief executive officer, and that was a square—a quadruple dominant profile. The reason is easy to understand. A CEO must deal with people who think in all four quadrants, and if she prefers to think in all four, then she can translate between them for all parties involved. The Herrmann people have found that these profiles occur only about 3 percent of the time, so we wouldn't expect to find many people in this category.

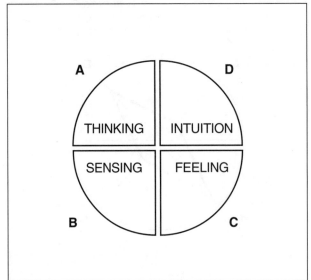

FIGURE 5.21 Correlation of HBDI with Myers-Briggs

Jim Lewis met one such individual, and sure enough, he was a turnaround CEO who specialized in saving hospitals from financial disaster. Unlike some individuals who specialize in turnarounds, this man tried to employ measures that saved as many jobs as possible. The turnaround CEO with very low C-Quadrant thinking is often concerned only with the bottom line, and thinks the quickest way to improve financial performance is to eliminate jobs, regardless of the cost in human suffering. Naturally he or she will justify such action by saying that sacrificing a few jobs is better for everyone in the long run. We did have the Herrmann group pull a composite profile for all of the project managers they had in their database, and the overall is

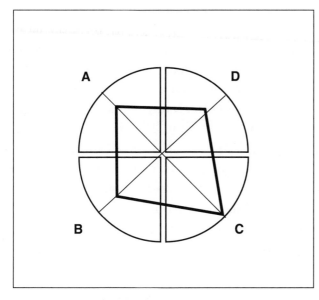

FIGURE 5.22 Profile of Female Project Managers

square. They had 1,250 profiles for project managers, with the population being almost perfectly split fifty-fifty between men and women. These profiles are shown in Figures 5.22 and 5.23. There is a small tilt toward the A-Quadrant for men, and a small tilt toward the C-Quadrant for women; this tilt was found as well in the profiles for project managers.

What this suggests is that project managers come in "all shapes and sizes." There has to be a fairly even distribution of profiles to get a composite square, so the distribution for project managers is not very different than for the population in general.

As has been stated, what the thinking preference of an individual will do is

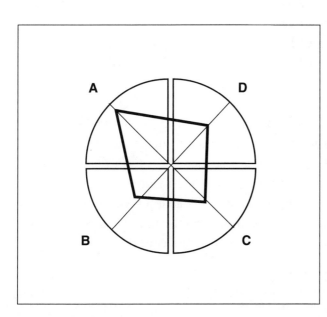

FIGURE 5.23 Profile of Male Project Managers

affect his "style" of managing projects. The one concern we would have about this would be with project managers who have very little preference for C-Quadrant thinking. The reason is that the age-old problem with project managers is that they have a lot of responsibility and very little authority, so the only way they can get anything done is through influence, negotiation, begging, and selling. Project managers with very low preference for the C-Quadrant are inclined to say, "I hate dealing with people problems." To these individuals we generally suggest they rethink whether they truly want to manage projects. This would be the one deficit we feel should enter into one's decision about whether to be a project manager. If you hate dealing with people, then why subject yourself to the daily agony that you are sure to experience as a project manager?

Kirton Innovation-Adaptive Profile*

Michael J. Kirton has studied the creative-thinking process and determined that it has two aspects to it: one is the *level* of the intellectual process, and the other is the *style* of problem-solving. Level has to do with one's intelligence, experience, and so on. Style, however, is of a single dimension, anchored on one end by innovators and on the other by adapters. Kirton contends that it is confusion between level and style that has caused so much difficulty in helping individuals develop their innovative or creative thinking ability.

Adapters, when confronted with a problem, tend to turn to conventional rules, practices, and perceptions of the group to which they belong. This can be a working group, cultural group, or professional or occupational group. They then derive their ideas from the established procedures of this group. If there is no ready-made answer provided by a collection of conventional responses, the adapter will try to adapt or stretch a conventional response until it can be used to solve the problem. Thus, much of the behavior of adapters is in the category of im-

---

* This material is adapted from *Mastering Project Management* by James P. Lewis. (McGraw-Hill © 1998, used by permission.)

proving existing methods, or "doing better" what is already done. This strategy, which tends to dominate management, has been exemplified since 1980 by the continuous improvement process advocated by Dr. Edwards Deming. The flaw in continuous improvement is that one eventually reaches a point at which a process should no longer be improved, but should be eliminated.

Innovation is the characteristic behavior of individuals who, when they have a problem, try to reorganize or restructure the problem and to approach it in a new light. In doing so, they try to divorce themselves from preconceived notions about the nature of the problem and its solution. Their approach can be called "doing things differently," instead of "doing things better."

Relationships Between Innovators and Adapters. Because of their different styles in solving problems, it can be expected that innovators and adapters might have conflicts on teams, and this is sometimes the case. Adapters tend to see innovators as abrasive, insensitive, and disruptive. They are always wanting to change things, always creating havoc. Innovators see adapters as stuffy and unenterprising. They are hung up on systems, rules, and norms of behavior that seem restrictive and ineffective to the adapters. So, when the extreme innovator meets the extreme adapter, sparks are likely to fly.

The Strong-Campbell Interest Inventory

The Strong-Campbell Interest Inventory is designed specifically for job or career counseling. The instrument assesses your interest in a wide range of topics and compares them to data from individuals who are in various careers. Presumably, if you have interests that are highly similar to those individuals who already occupy a particular profession, this profession may well be your "calling." What the instrument does not do is assess one's *ability* to do that job. So if you have interests very similar to that of musicians, you will not likely be successful as a musician unless you have musical talent.

What Are You Motivated to Do?   There are many theories of motivation, but they all tend to focus on how we satisfy needs. Abraham Maslow's hierarchy of needs is one example, and it says that we have needs that fall into five categories: biological, safety/security, social, self-esteem, and self-actualization. So the idea is that we try to help employees satisfy their various needs through their work, because they are already motivated to satisfy those needs, and if they can do so through the job, then we will get top performance from them. Unfortunately, it can be very difficult to pinpoint what specific needs will motivate the person, so the models have been somewhat unhelpful to the practicing manager.

There is another facet of motivation that has received less attention, and that has relevance to you in your search for the best career. People are also motivated to engage in various patterns of activity, and seek these out and are most happy and content when they can do the things they love to do.

Some of these patterns of activity are labelled as follows:

- Expert. A person with this pattern enjoys learning new things and being asked by people to share that knowledge.
- Innovator. The individual who has a strong drive to be innovative is probably a D-Quadrant thinker. These individuals thrive on developing new ideas, new products, new artistic creations, etc.
- Defender. This individual thrives on maintaining compliance with rules and regulations. In terms of Keirsey's temperaments, he or she is probably an SJ, as well as a B-Quadrant thinker.
- Troubleshooter. People with this pattern are challenged to fix things that are broken. They love to match wits with difficult problems.
- Helper. As the name implies, such individuals like to be helpful to others. In terms of temperament, they most likely are NF idealists.

Again, we would expect that a person with any motivation pattern could be effective as a project manager, but would engage in the job in terms of his or her pattern of motivation. For example, the defender would be concerned that people follow the project plan to the letter, never deviating. This might be desirable in some situations, but for projects that have a more unstable nature, trying to follow a plan rigidly could be counterproductive. If you have such a motivation pattern, you would be advised to avoid such projects, or you will make yourself and your team members unhappy.

The ideal, then, would be for you to seek out projects that would allow you to maximize your work in terms of your motivation pattern. In doing so, you will be most productive and most rewarded. So the question is, how do you determine your pattern?

The Self-analysis Process

In this process, there are three questions you ask yourself. We suggest that you either write out your responses or else tape-record them. Here they are:

1. Describe a job you have had that you really "got into." You put a large amount of energy into it, loved doing so, couldn't wait to get to work each day, and you found the day going by rapidly. What was your role in this job? What did you like most about it? If you wanted to sell someone else on doing this same job, what would you tell them?
2. Pick some outside activity that you really enjoy doing. It can be a hobby or sport, but it must be an activity, not an escape from stress such as lying on a beach vegetating. It is helpful to pick one that you would engage in more frequently if you had more time. What do you like about this activity? If you wanted to convince someone who was interested in the activity that it would be fun, what would you tell that person?
3. Now think into the future. Most of us have something in mind that we have not yet done in life but would like to do sometime. This might be called your wish list or fantasy list. Assume for a moment that you could do one of these things. What would it be? How would you go about it? For example, people sometimes

Discover your
motivation pattern.

---

say they would like to travel. Would it be out of the country? Would you want to see buildings, the countryside, or get to know the people? Would you want to immerse yourself in a certain area for several days, or hit five cities in three days?

Analysis.   When you have completed answering the three questions, go back over them, review them, and look for the common thread that runs through them. You will find there is a pattern of activity that is common to all three. If you can't find it, share the data with someone else and ask them to help. This is often a good activity for an A-Quadrant thinker, as it requires analytical thinking. If you still can't find the pattern, go back to question two and answer it for another outside activity. Or you can repeat questions one and three. The reason for suggesting that you redo question two is because our outside activities are where many of us put the most energy, and which

we enjoy most. In fact, we have given you maximum flexibility by using the three categories of work, play, and fantasy. You could get the pattern from three examples in any single category.

Once you know your motivation pattern, you can be more proactive in seeking jobs that are a good fit for you. And you will find your work experience much more rewarding than it may have been up to now.

Summary

There are clearly a lot of factors to consider in looking at your own career and how you stack up against the requirements of the job. We hope you don't find it overwhelming, but if you do, you may want to consult a career counselor and share your findings with him or her so you can sort through it all. The interpretation of the large mass of data can be intimidating, and a professional counselor can be a big help. It's a big step, and one that you want to take with as much care as possible.

chapter 6

What Kind of Job Environment Are You In?

Introduction

If you really want to be successful as a project manager, you must understand the environment in which you work. That means knowing what it is and, more importantly, knowing how to survive and thrive in it. In this chapter we are going to prepare you for every organizational environment we can think of. You will not only understand how each organizational structure works, you will also learn what the pitfalls are, the advantages the structure offers, and how to develop a winning strategy for each environment you might encounter.

We are now ready to take a look at the more common structures you will encounter.

The Functional Structure

This organizational structure is an archetype of the industrial age. It is partially or totally being replaced by other more resource-efficient or customer-focused structures such as some form of a matrix or hybrid structure.

This type of organization divides responsibility among business functions (see Figure 6.1). Departments are formed for each business

You
must
understand
your job
environment.

function and are staffed by managers, professionals, and administrative personnel, whose business skills are limited to those that are directly related to the business function that defines their unit. Projects have little visibility in these organizations. A given project may be managed by someone in each functional area when it is their turn to work on the project. As a result, no one really understands the entire project, and the whole process of completing a project takes too long. The business function department's people understand the work they have to do on a project, but have little understanding of the project beyond the boundaries of their business discipline. The risk of project failure is very high. On the positive side, the functional structure is very efficient in the use of resources. Such organizations are generally good at producing products and providing services but are traditionally not good at solving enterprise-wide problems. The only projects that work

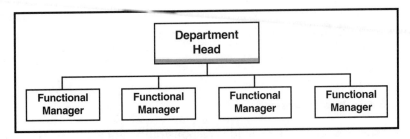

FIGURE 6.1   Functional organization

in these structures are single-department projects or projects that can be decomposed into sub-projects that require little integration or cross-department collaboration.

What Does This Mean to the Development of a Project Manager?

There are still a number of companies that are primarily organized along functional lines, so it is worth spending some time assessing this organization as it impacts on project manager career development. As a project manager, you are trapped within the functional area in which you are employed. That means your development opportunities are limited to the projects that arise within that function. At the entry level you are a team leader and the opportunities for development will be present, but as you begin to develop your project management skills the lack of opportunity for further sophistication

> **As a project manager, you are trapped within the functional area in which you are employed. That means your develoment opportunities are limited . . .**

and growth will dwindle. Within a single function, project scope and complexity is limited—so don't look for the WOW Project. It won't be there.

The Matrix Structure

This type of organization divides responsibility along two lines: along business functions, and along projects. Your first question should be: "Doesn't that leave room for politics and power struggles?" And your second question should be: "Won't I get caught in the middle?" The answer to both questions is, "It depends," but there is good news in this answer.

In general, the matrix structure has professional staff reporting to a business unit (usually a business function at a department or subdepartment level). Project managers draw their team members from the business units. Individual professional staff are usually assigned to more than one project at a time. The project manager does not have line authority over their team members, but they are responsible for getting the work of the project done

> **. . . the matrix structure need not be enterprise-wide.**

through these team members. It might help to think of the staff member's business function manager as being responsible for managing the person, and the project manager being responsible for managing the work that the person does. This relationship between managing people and managing work draws upon the leadership skills of the project manager more than it does upon their people management skills.

There are three types of variations on the matrix structure. Each brings a different set of challenges, and each offers different opportunities for you as project manager or team member looking for skill development. It is important to understand that the matrix structure need not be enterprise-wide. Its use may, in fact, be determined by the importance of the project to the organization or the importance of the project as compared to the importance of the business functions that staff projects. Let's take a look at each one.

The Weak Matrix

Figure 6.2 illustrates the weak matrix structure. Note here that the business function dominates. What this means is that the functional managers decide priorities and what resources will be allocated to which projects. In the weak matrix structure, projects are not as critical or important to the organization as the business functions that deploy staff to projects. Although the weak matrix provides more development opportunities than the function structure, the strong and balanced matrix structures provide even better opportunities.

The Strong Matrix

Figure 6.3 illustrates the strong matrix structure. Note here that the project manager dominates. What this means is that the project priorities are determined by the senior manager or management team charged with stewardship of the project portfolio. The business functional managers have two separate responsibilities: development and deployment.

> **... the functional managers decide priorities and what resources will be allocated to which projects.**

Development Responsibilities of Functional Managers

Their development responsibility requires that they are knowledgeable of the demand for project managers and team members in terms of the skill profiles required of current and future projects. They must then identify their training needs and implement programs to that effect. Not all

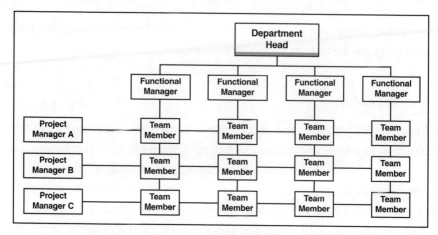

FIGURE 6.2   The Weak Matrix Organization

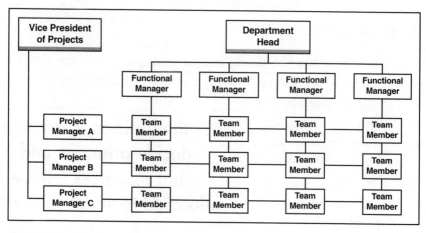

FIGURE 6.3   The Strong Matrix Organization

training requires the attendee to buy plane tickets and hotel rooms. In many cases they can use projects as on-the-job training programs as well.

Deployment Responsibilities of Functional Managers

The deployment responsibilities of functional managers require that they be knowledgeable of the skill requirements of a project and deploy staff according to the project time line. This can happen in two stages. During the planning stage, they might be required to commit to meeting specific skill requirements within a specific window of time. For example, they may commit to providing database analyst skills for ten hours per week from July 1 through August 31. It is not necessary to identify the specific person or persons who will meet this need. That comes in the second phase. As the time approaches to actually schedule a person or persons to the project, the choice will be made by the functional managers. This may involve some negotiation with the project manager.

The Balanced Matrix

Figure 6.4 illustrates the balanced matrix structure. In this type of structure, the project managers and the business function managers are on equal turf. Since neither dominates,

> **Project priorities are determined by the senior manager . . . charged with stewardship of the project portfolio.**

this structure sets up a negotiating situation for the project manager and the function manager. Because of this, this structure is far more politically charged than the weak or strong matrix variations.

How to Handle Being Both a Functional Manager and a Project Manager

A particularly difficult situation arises when a functional manager will have responsibility for a project that is entirely contained within her business unit. Being a project manager in this situation has one great advantage: You are both the project manager for the team and the line manager for the team members. In other

> **In this type of structure, the project managers and the business function managers are on equal turf.**

The functional manager deploys staff according to skill and time line.

words, you own the staff resources that are assigned to the project. Sounds great, doesn't it? But, wait, there is a trap waiting to be sprung. Simply put, how do you decide which of your staff to assign to your project and which to assign to projects outside of your functional area?

... appeal to project priorities established elsewhere.

What projects have priority? To which projects will you assign your most skilled staff? Since you are a project manager, you will want the best-qualified staff you can get for your project. However, if you use that strategy, you may be accused of not being a team player by the other project managers. The reverse strategy isn't so good, either. By assigning your best staff to the other projects, you put your project at risk. The only way out of this dilemma is to appeal to project priorities established elsewhere or the criticality of the activities to which the staff are to be assigned.

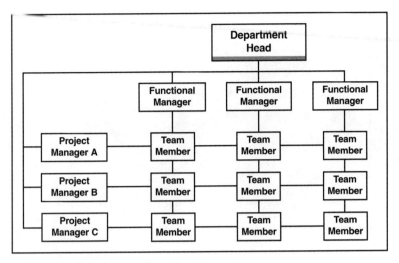

FIGURE 6.4   The Balanced Matrix Organization

What Does This Mean to the Development of a Project Manager?

There are several advantages that the matrix structure provides for you as you look for further development of your project management skills and career. First, the matrix offers better assessment of skill and development needs. This responsibility is vested in your functional manager. Feedback from your project manager or from the manager of project managers will address your performance and further development needs. Second, you have a range of projects to choose from as you look for on-the-job development situations. Third, you can move from simpler to more complex project assignments as you acquire the appropriate skills.

The Project Structure

Figure 6.5 illustrates the project structure. This form is used almost exclusively in government-related projects and some long-term commercial ventures. Here the project team has a line relationship with the project manager. They are assigned full-time to one project. When the

GOAL

As a team member you are confined to the boundaries of the project.

project is completed or canceled, they are reassigned to another project.

... it is not very conducive to the development of special skills, and no clear career paths emerge.

While this structure is beneficial to and supportive of the practice of good project management, it is not very conducive to the development of special skills, and no clear career paths emerge. As a team member you are confined to the boundaries of the project and are only expected to contribute your current expertise to the project. You were chosen for the team because of your skills.

What Does This Mean to the Development of a Project Manager?

At first glance this might seem to be the best of all worlds, but it isn't. Unlike a matrix structure, you will be assigned to one project at a time. Your assignment is more likely based on the technical skills you already possess than on any need for further development. When you reach the level of senior project manager, you can begin to look for those WOW Project assignments and professional growth beyond the

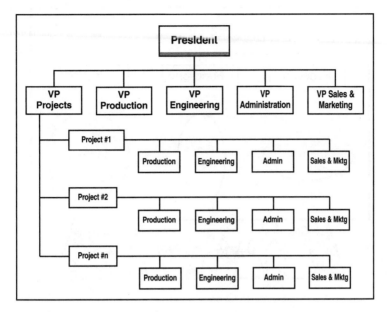

FIGURE 6.5   Project Form of Organization

level of project manager to program manager or into general management or consulting.(See the discussion of WOW Projects later in this chapter.)

The Self-directed Team Structure

Figure 6.6 illustrates the self-directed team structure. These structures tend to be permanent ones whose scope of responsibility is usually a business process or function. The key to their development value to you lies in the fact that they are self-contained. That is, they must possess the skills needed to accomplish their objectives. If they don't have the skills they must either recruit someone who does, or develop them among one or more of their current team members. If you are on such a team, look for opportunities to develop a needed skill that the team has recognized it needs. In the absence of those opportunities, the self-directed team does not offer a great deal in the way of devlopment opportunities.

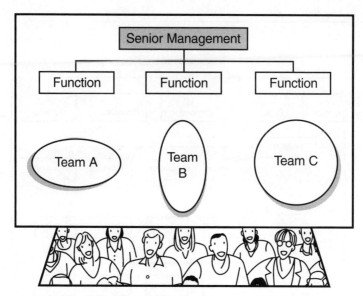

FIGURE 6.6   Self-directed Organization

What Does This Mean to the Development of a Project Manager?

There are a lot of similarities between the project form and the self-directed or task force structure. Self-directed teams tend to be permanent. If so, you are limited to the development opportunities that lie within the scope of the team. This is similar to the limitations placed on you in the functional organization. The self-directed team differs in one respect: It is self-contained. That means it has all of the skills and expertise it needs to succeed. If it doesn't, it must develop them, and here is where you will find opportunities that go beyond those of the functional structure.

> **If you are on such a team, look for opportunities to develop a needed skill that the team has recognized it needs.**

Centers of Excellence

Within a business function a number of centers of excellence may have been established. Their purpose is to provide a service to the organization through the development and deployment of qualified staff to meet a specific organizational need. The most frequent centers of excellence are found in the information technology departments of organizations. Centers of excellence may be defined for a specific hardware and/or software environment. Each center would be staffed by subject matter experts who serve as team members or consultants to the project team.

Career Development and Organizational Structures

Now that we have defined and discussed the various organizational forms you are likely to encounter, we can consider strategies and tactics you will need to employ in order for you to grow professionally in each environment. To get started, let us take a look from 60,000 feet above a model of organizational structures and look at how project management fares in that model. Figure 6.7 presents organizations on a continuum beginning with functional and evolving through weak and strong matrix types to the pure project form. Along that continuum, project management ranges from nonexistent to dominant. The graph measures the extent to which that structure provides development opportunities for those who are or wish to be project managers. Depending on the environment you work in, you get a broad picture of your opportunities. Every structure provides opportunities for professional development, but some present more than others.

How Does This Relate to Your Career?

You will have noted that the type of organizational structure within which you work will either be a help or a hindrance to your career development efforts. If it is a help, you will be able to move your career

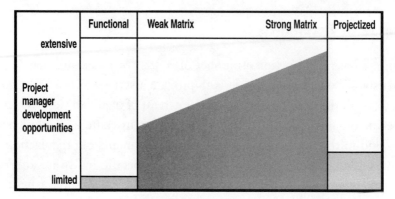

FIGURE 6.7   Development Opportunities by Organizational Structure

forward with mutual support from the organization, your manager, and the project managers with whom you work. If it is a hindrance, you will have to look inward and draw upon your own creativity and initiative in order to move your career forward. In time you may find that the hindrances are overwhelming and you are unable to progress as a project manager. You then have a decision to make. Is the job more important or is career advancement more important? If the career is more important, it is time to move on.

Fortunately, the matrix structure, which is the most common structure you will encounter, offers the best opportunities for professional development. Let's take a closer look at exactly what we mean.

In the weak matrix structure the functional manager controls the assignment of her staff to projects that she is supporting. Your strategy will be to make sure that your manager knows about your career goals, or more specifically about your short-term skill development needs.

In the case of the strong matrix structure the situation is quite different but in a positive sense. Your functional manager will be responsible for development and deployment and will certainly be of help in placing you in the appropriate assignment, but there is another opportunity the strong matrix structure presents: the project itself. This means you can and should seek out projects that provide opportunities for you to meet your development needs. In other words, in the weak matrix structure you are primarily in a passive mode (your manager calls the shots), while in the strong matrix structure you can add an active mode (you reach

Fortunately, the matrix structure . . . offers the best opportunities for professional development.

out and try to get on the right projects). This has shades of the WOW Project written about by Tom Peters. We strongly recommend that you study what he has to say.

"WOW" projects add value, leave a legacy.

According to Peters, WOW Projects are "projects that add value, projects that matter, projects that make a difference, projects that leave a legacy—and, yes, projects that make you a star." Peters offers a few rules that will help you think about projects in the right way. They are

1. Projects are a way for the powerless to gain power.
2. Projects are a way for the company to discover its future.
3. Projects should never be allowed to grow dreary.
4. Project managers should draft people like a general manager and invest like a venture capitalist.

Let's examine each of these rules and focus on their relevance to your career development.

1. **Projects are a way for the powerless to gain power.** Nothing contributes to success like success. If you have ever been successful at anything you did, you will of course remember the exhilaration you felt at the time, but do you remember that another opportunity to be even more successful was presented shortly thereafter? Probably not, since you were still congratulating yourself over the recent victory. If you pay attention, you can leverage one success to help produce another. That is the way for you to move your career forward. All it takes is paying attention so you can recognize and seize those opportunities.

> **If you pay attention, you can leverage one success to help produce another.**

2. **Projects are a way for the company to discover its future.** Regardless of the outcome of your current project, learning will take place. In addition to the company discovering its future, you will discover yours. You have to begin thinking about projects as stepping stones along your career path. Some will move you forward as planned, while others will give you reason to stop and reconsider your next step. Do not miss an opportunity to extract this benefit from every project.

3. **Projects should never be allowed to grow dreary.** No matter how mundane a project may seem, always look for the diamond in the rough. Some of that value may come in the form of lessons learned that you will want to carry forward in your project work, while others will come in the form of actions to be avoided. Real learning takes place when you make mistakes and adjust your future behavior as a result.

4. **Project managers should draft people like a general manager and invest like a venture capitalist.** As a project manager, you want to give yourself every opportunity to be successful. That

means getting the right people and assigning them to the right job. Recruit to your weaknesses and use that as an opportunity to correct those weaknesses. Several years ago Bob Wysocki, as head of computing for his company, learned an important lesson about commitment from his manager, Ed, the president of the company. Ed said, "Bob, spend your budget as though you were spending your own money." If you think about it that way, you have the right level of commitment.

How to Make WOW Projects Happen

WOW Projects are certainly a key to your future, so you might ask how to make them happen. Peters offers four steps.

Step one: Take the "Does it matter?" test. You are not going to move ahead in your career by working on projects that simply have no value to the organization or, as Peters says, simply don't make a difference. Why is that the case? Projects that don't matter can come and go with the rise and fall of business. But projects that do matter will have some staying power with senior management—in other words, they are less likely to be cancelled and therefore are more likely to give you a chance to learn and be successful from having had the opportunity to manage them.

Step two: No project is too mundane to become a WOW Project. Here, Peters is saying be creative. Look for the hidden opportunities that every project contains. For example, you might want to expand or redirect the scope of the project to include deliverables from which you can extract value. If you can sell management on the new scope or at least create an opportunity within the present scope that you can work to your advantage, you have found a way to turn the project into a WOW Project.

Step three: To a real life-in-the-project person everything is a good learning opportunity. This step is best illustrated with an example from Bob Wysocki. The lesson came from his manager, Ed, the president, whom we cited earlier in the chapter. Whenever Bob was discussing a problem with Ed, he always presented two or three alternative ways of solving the problem, along with the advantages and disadvantages of each. Almost without exception Ed would reject them all and say something like, "Bob, you haven't considered all of the possibilities. What if you combined your first and second alternatives? Get back to me when you have something better to offer."

> **"spend your budget as though you were spending your own money."**

As it turns out, this was nothing more than a delay tactic Ed used when he didn't want to deal with the problem. Bob knew that, but he learned a valuable lesson from the experience, in any case. And that lesson was to ask yourself if you really have considered all alternatives. Maybe by combining two of them you get a third alternative that is even better.

Step four: Use super-fast approximations to refine your WOW Project. The trick here is to get results as quickly as possible. You are not demonstrating value to the organization by working on projects that won't see the light of day for several quarters or years. Get something out, start getting payback early, and use those early successes to parlay the project into a sequence of projects that eventually lead to the WOW Project. The risk is too high that a project of longer duration will never come about, since business conditions change every Tuesday and longer duration projects get killed in the flurry of that change.

> **Look for the hidden opportunities that every project contains.**

Summary

We have shared our wisdom and experiences with you regarding organizational structures and how they can help or hinder. You now know what to look for regardless of the type of organization you work for.

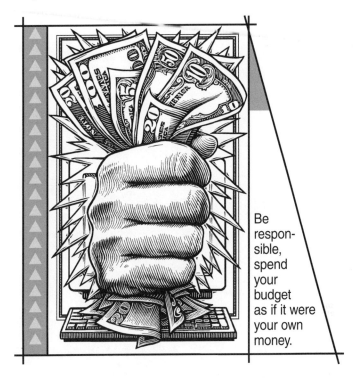

Be respon- sible, spend your budget as if it were your own money.

Each structure presents opportuni- ties—you just need to find them and then act on them. In the next chap- ter we have a treat in store for you. Our colleague, Doug DeCarlo, is a recognized expert in reading and

... ask yourself if you really have considered all alternatives.

acting on the realities of organizations when it comes to surviving in the jungle, as he puts it. Doug graciously accepted our offer to write Chapter Seven. We're glad he did!

chapter 7

It's a Jungle in Here

How to Survive and Thrive in
Today's Project-crazy Organizations

DOUG DECARLO*

Projects are difficult. They are high stress. And when we walk out of
the office, they come home with us at night, often as uninvited guests
who live rent-free in our heads.

Many project managers who work in high velocity, complex, and
demanding project environments are experiencing a deteriorating
quality of life, both at work and at home.

Yet the teachings of project management don't extend beyond the
walls of our offices, although our projects do. The project management
profession focuses on expanding its body of project knowledge by
identifying best practices, developing new methodologies, and creating software tools to enable us to make a success out of the projects we
are asked to undertake.

---

* This chapter is an outcome of Doug's career over the last thirty-two years in the
business community. For the last seven years he has worked with more than 150
project teams, from Beijing, China, to Bethlehem, Pennsylvania. During that
time, as a senior project management consultant with the ICS Group, Doug was
in the trenches with project managers, project sponsors, and senior managers as a
teacher, consultant, coach, and facilitator on a wide range of projects, including
information technology, e-commerce, research and development, process

In the meantime, project managers are being left emotionally bankrupt by the demands placed on them. Many of the project managers we know harbor the unspoken hope "If I can just put together the right combination of tools and techniques, I will at last be able to get my projects under control and my life back to normal."

Yet, we never seem to get there. We are digging a hole for ourselves. We have fallen into the trap of all traps: thinking that doing more of what doesn't work will, someday, eventually work.

But how do you get out of that hole? The first thing to do is stop digging. Recognize that the most important project we face is the one that stares back at us with hopeful eyes every morning when we look in the mirror.

The place to begin is by placing the spotlight on ourselves as the main event. To be truly effective, we must reclaim ourselves before we can reclaim our projects. We begin to reclaim ourselves by recognizing that a high quality of life is *not* a destination. It's the starting point, a place to come from, rather than to go to. It's our mind-set as we step into the jungle. It's a choice we make. There are no prerequisites.

The goal of this chapter, which will later be expanded into a book, is to put in place the fundamental building blocks essential to enjoying a high quality life both on and off the job.

The three insights and ten lessons of the "jungle" that form the heart of this chapter serve as a template that enables us to develop both self-mastery and project mastery. The three insights are overarching principles, which form the fundamental mind-set for success. In contrast, the ten lessons are practices that provide actionable approaches to improve one's quality of life. Each lesson is applied on the personal level, and then extended to the project level.

reengineering, continuous improvement, sales generation, and new product introductions, with budgets ranging from $25,000 to over $25 million.

Doug is the founder of The Doug DeCarlo Group, which develops new approaches that work in project environments where the rules of traditional project management no longer apply. The Group provides services to project managers, sponsors, and teams who want to take action to excel in both business performance and in overall quality of life.

You Haven't Seen Anything Yet

As we move into the twenty-first century, even greater demands will be placed on project managers and team leaders to do more, go faster, and use fewer resources to get the job done. Fueled by accelerating competitive forces, rapid changes in technology, along with the demands for speed and innovation in the new e-commerce economy, the pressure on project managers and team members to perform will only escalate. These challenges will be compounded by the quickening pace and complexities associated with globalization. And, as project teams become increasingly more dispersed and diverse, it is becoming especially difficult to manage the all-important people side or "soft side" of the project.

The Project-crazy Organization

The reality is that within this chaotic and demanding world of projects, our own organizations may not provide an environment that makes our project life as easy as we'd like. In fact, it is quite common nowadays to work in what might be called a downright project-unfriendly organization, one that has seemingly worked hard to establish a series of entrenched worst practices. Here are just a few examples:

- **Priorities**
  "Project du jour" is the rule, where no accepted criteria for project selection are in place.
- **Communications**
  "Mushroom management" is practiced, where team members are kept in the dark on issues that impact the scope and quality of deliverables; this results in re-work, and animosity.
- **Team stability**
  The revolving door. Team members come and go as they are reassigned to new projects du jour.

The pressure is on to perform.

- **Roles**
  Who has what decisionmaking authority is unclear, resulting in
  the project sponsor and functional managers pulling the project
  in different directions while the project leader holds on for dear
  life.
- **Project Management**
  No consistent, common methodology is in place. Project
  influencers like to increase scope while decreasing resources and
  shortening the schedule.
- **Reward System**
  You get to keep your job.

This hypothetical organizational profile is all too typical. And it has
consequences at both the business and personal levels:

- Greater risk of project failure due to organizational factors
- Greater demands on the project manager's well-being and
  quality of life

Our Heroes: Methodology and Technology?

Navigating one's way through the project jungle in these exciting yet difficult times is a real challenge. What makes it especially challenging is that we have been taught to look for answers in the wrong places.

Nowadays, a common approach to taming the project jungle is to energetically bring in new project management methodologies, along with their supporting technologies. We look to the latest advances in group ware, team ware, and project management software to get us through the jungle, only to find that these are not the panaceas we thought. Mastery of project management technologies and methodologies may facilitate the project manager's safari, but alone will not provide safe passage. All too often we are finding that the people part of the "technology, process, people" equation is the showstopper, the variable that is invariably left out. And, when we find that methodology and technology are not taking hold, we tend to step up the pace. The motto seems to be, " If it ain't working, let's do more of it." Doing more of what doesn't work can make things worse.

So, What Do We Do? What Is the Goal? And How Do We Begin?

At day's end, if the project is a resounding success but our personal, family, and work lives are emotionally bankrupt, what have we gained?

We begin by going back to the beginning and asking ourselves, what do we truly want? A successful project? Is that what we live for? When it comes down to it, the bottom line for most people is to enjoy a satisfactory quality of life, both work life as well as personal life. But how do we achieve this? Do we have to wait until the organization is cured of its project craziness?

A fundamental and age-old insight, translated into jungle parlance, shouts out to us: "It's not the jungle we have to tame, it's ourselves."

And how do we do that?

It's not the jungle we have to tame, it's ourselves

These exigencies and challenges of the new millennium will put a premium on our ability to go back to basics and to redirect our energies to focus on those things that are within our power to change. The fact is, we can't change the competitive scene, the course of globalization, or that projects will become increasingly complex. What can we change? To borrow a concept from Stephen Covey's book, *The 7 Habits of Highly Successful People*, the place to start is to clearly understand the difference between one's circle of concern versus one's circle of influence, and to devote our energies to the latter.

In my own personal area of no concern are some things I could care less about:

- Politics in Ecuador
- Golf
- Oprah

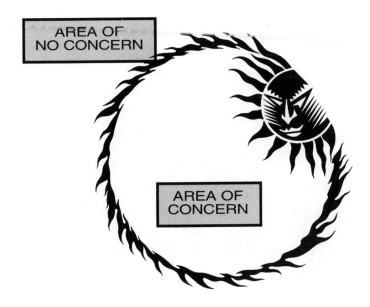

Included inside my circle of concern are things over which I have a great deal of interest, but little or no ability to change:

- The stock market
- The weather
- My organization's project-unfriendly culture
- What my competitors are doing
- Technology changes
- What my children do with their lives

All too often, project team leaders and their teams fall into the "jungle" trap of bemoaning and dwelling upon those realities that are outside their sphere of influence. When a team starts to act this way, it begins to give up its power to get things done. Why? Because unless

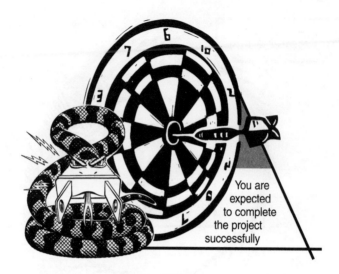

and until that something outside of the team changes, the team feels powerless (literally has less power) to do the job.

The focus of the team's energies then shifts to things over which it can do little or nothing. And, because what we focus upon expands (e.g., negativity), that becomes the dominant energy surrounding the project. By taking a reactive approach, the team soon adopts a defeatist attitude as its modus operandi, which in turn becomes a self-fulfilling prophecy, with finger pointing and endless complaining about how dysfunctional management is.

I refer to this as responding with disability, the opposite of taking responsibility (i.e., responding with ability). However, at the end of the day, the team is still expected to complete the project successfully, no matter how unfriendly we might think the organization is.

The key to all of this is to not lose sight of one's circle of influence, or those areas over which one can have a direct impact. A few examples include:

- Your health
- Your bank account
- Your relationships with friends and family

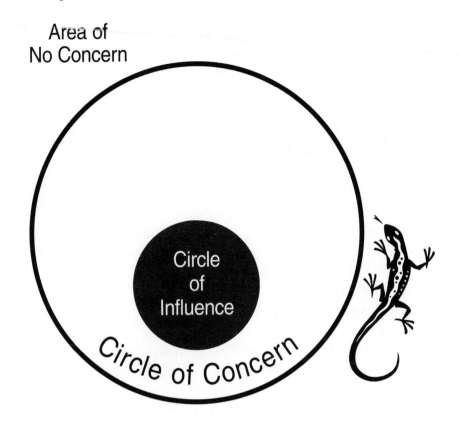

- Personal stress
- Gaining commitment and mutual accountability among team members
- How you *respond* to events over which you have no control
- Certain risks on the project that can be mitigated

The Goal Is to Expand One's Circle of Influence

The successful team leader will continually focus the team's energies on those areas where the team is power*ful* (and not power*less*). This, then, is the proactive approach, which expands the team's circle of influence and drives out negative (reactive) energy and improves the likelihood of success. In this model of the project world, the team leader sees him or herself as, first and foremost, a manager of energy, one whose job is to unblock the team's ability to move forward.

The Serenity Prayer sums it up nicely:

God, give us grace to accept with serenity
the things that cannot be changed,
courage to change the things
which should be changed,
and the wisdom to distinguish
the one from the other.
Living one day at a time,
Enjoying one moment at a time,
Accepting hardship as a pathway to peace,
Taking, as Jesus did,
This sinful world as it is,
Not as I would have it,
Trusting that You will make all things right,
If I surrender to Your will,
So that I may be reasonably happy in this life,
And supremely happy with You forever in the next.
Amen.

Reinhold Niebuhr (1892–1971)

Expanding one's circle of influence means mastering the inner game of project management. The three insights and ten lessons of the jungle are vehicles to do just that. These put the spotlight on the mind-set, attitudes, and internal qualities that project managers and their teams will need to adopt in order to prosper in the project jungle, while sidestepping both project and personal quicksand.

The Three Insights and Ten Lessons of the Jungle

These insights and lessons serve as a template for not only surviving, but for thriving. They empower the team leader and the team to move ahead with clarity and speed, despite external circumstances.

The three insights are overarching, guiding principles. They serve as a mental model, a set of lenses, if not philosophies, for seeing the world in an inspiring way. The insights provide the context for the ten lessons. If the insights are where the rubber meets the sky, the ten lessons are where the rubber meets the road. These are the tactics, providing specific, actionable techniques and approaches to improve one's quality of life on both the personal level and at the project level as well.

The successful project manager and team leader will devote time to achieve self-mastery, a prerequisite for effective leadership.

The First Insight: Prosperity Is a Choice

Given the complexities of projects and the associated high-risk factors, a team leader can easily feel overwhelmed and over her head, with no clear path in sight to get through the jungle. It's easy to adopt a fatality or scarcity mind-set such as "I'll be happy to get out of this one alive."

Jim McGrane, a very energetic and excellent advertising sales manager who worked for me at one time, came into the office one Friday after being on the road for a week. He was having a hard time getting computer companies to buy advertising space in our new magazine, despite his heroic efforts and those of his sales staff.

Jim said, "Selling advertising in this magazine is like beating your head against the wall. The good thing is that when you stop, it feels good." Jim had fallen into the jungle trap of believing that the best he could do was alleviate pain. And when this mind-set becomes one's dominant way of seeing the world and life in general, it also becomes the default setting for our internal computer. We develop a scarcity mentality, which in turn leads to a low expectation of life and a philosophy of "I'll cut my losses." As Stephen Covey and his circles remind us, what we dwell upon expands. If we focus on scarcity, at the very best, we end up going through life, day in and day out, practicing negative motivation—that is, focusing on keeping bad from happening. And that is not the formula for an inspired life.

A team that starts off feeling half-defeated or is running scared greatly increases the risk of never getting the project done successfully.

Given the complexity of projects, a team leader can feel over-whelmed.

Prosperity-thinking is a mind-set rather than a destination to be reached. It's the starting place, a place to come from, the upfront outlook going into the day, going into a project. It's an inner knowing that "I am, and deserve to be, prosperous no matter what the outcome of the project, even if the project fails."

Put another way, it's just another default setting on our internal computer. It's a choice. We either click on "prosperity mentality" or on "scarcity mentality." Pick one. Then act that way.

But we need help in clicking. That's where the ten lessons come into play.

Lesson #1: Discover Your Life's Purpose.   Nathaniel Branden, the pre-eminent psychologist who specializes in the psychology of self-esteem, makes the point that we all have a heroic mission to fulfill. Our heroic mission is the unique contribution each of us wants to make to the world, how we want to be of service. This intrinsic desire to want to make a difference, coupled with the discovery of our own unique talent, is the foundation for living an inspired, meaningful life.

When a person is living with purpose, he goes through the day with a feeling of fulfillment, of being centered, seeing himself as making a difference in daily interactions. When we lose sight of our life's purpose, we tend to flounder and feel frustrated, incomplete, and drained.

*My purpose is to work with individuals and teams in
a way that achieves extraordinary results.*

One's purpose is one's path, as opposed to a destination or goal to be reached. People often confuse purpose and goals.

Goals play an important role. They are milestones along the path of living one's purpose.

People who are only goal oriented but have no underlying purpose for their life tend to feel fulfilled only when they achieve a goal, (e.g., a new Porsche). But the feeling is only temporary and typically leaves one vacant. The euphoria soon wears off just like the initial flavor of chewing gum doesn't last very long. A goal orientation in the absence of an underlying purpose leads to striving behavior, picking more aggressive goals in the hopes of finally experiencing permanent fulfillment. The result: being in a state of striving and never arriving and never feeling fulfilled in between the goals.

Once we discover what our purpose is, it's important to pick the appropriate vehicle—call it your job—in order to express that purpose. For instance, if your purpose in life was to quench the thirst of the desert dwellers, you wouldn't pick a sieve to transport the water.

Teaching, consulting, coaching, facilitating, and public speaking in the field of project management, team leadership, and personal mastery are the vehicles I use to deliver on my purpose.

A worthy undertaking, and maybe the most important undertaking of all, is to get in touch with your own purpose for being alive.

One way to discover your life's purpose is to take some time alone and reflect on those life experiences where you felt really good about having accomplished something or about having made a difference.

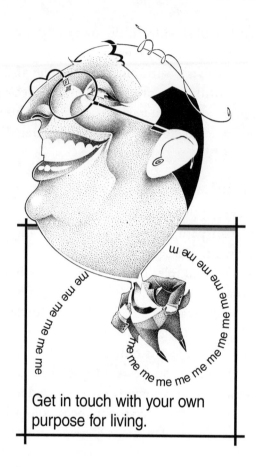

Get in touch with your own
purpose for living.

Look for the common denominators. When you start to see the pattern, fill in the following sentence:

"My reason for being alive is to:

"

For the Project Team

Many project teams flounder for months when they do not have clarity of purpose. That's why it is crucial for a team to reach consensus at the outset as to just what it thinks it is doing, and to express this in the form of a mission statement. A mission statement format, recommended by the ICS Group, a project management consulting firm, consists of two sentences. The first sentence answers three questions:

- Who are we?
- What is the expected project deliverable or result?
- For whom is the project conducted; that is, who is the project's customer?

The second sentence answers the question: Why are we doing this project? This is where the business case or rationale for the project is summed up. The first project manager was Noah, who was asked to head up the first right-sizing project. Using the two-sentence mission statement structure, Noah and his team might have come up with the following:

Noah and family will build an ark for the chosen ones. This supports the Sponsor's objective to start over with a whole new team.

Lesson #2: Create an Uplifting Vision.   There are a lot of definitions for "vision." A description that I have found useful is to think of a vision as a set of thoughts, mental pictures, and feelings about some future state; a description of what it looks and feels like when one is living in a state of peak performance and fulfillment.

This is what a world-class skier does when he creates a mental movie of gliding flawlessly down the slopes to victory to a standing ovation of fans gone wild. It means being a legend in your own mind. A vision means pre-experiencing the successful outcome of what you are after. Once we have a solid vision in place, an invisible hand seems to take over, and we begin to unconsciously select those people and experiences that lead us to our destination, even in the absence of a detailed plan.

Visioning is very powerful. It is a key step in manifesting and bringing into being what we want in life. In the absence of an inspiring vision, you have no filter to decide what to put into your Palm Pilot. And trivia will prevail.

For the Project Team

Just as an individual benefits from having a personal vision, so does a project team. One of the most powerful exercises for a team to undertake is to develop a vision statement.

The vision statement

- Enables the team to preexperience success.
- Builds commitment and enthusiasm.

How?
Ask team members to answer these questions:

If this project were successful beyond your wildest imagination, what would the impact be on the organization? On our customers? On the competition? On our industry? On the quality of our work life? On our personal life? On the world?

Capture their responses as part of the project kickoff process.

If time permits, responses can be discussed and combined into a short vision statement. Express the vision in the present tense, as if it has already been achieved.

Lesson #3: Embrace Fear.   Left unchecked, our fears will run rampant, and overpower, if not obliterate, our vision.

Because every project is a new venture, there is risk associated with the endeavor, both personal risk and business risk. Fear of making a mistake, fear of complete failure on the project, fear of being fired, even fear of success can haunt project managers and team members. All are very natural emotions, forever part of the human condition.

Fears are not easy for people to face. As a result, the responses to fear can include squelching, outright denial, rationalization, and the attitude of "kill the messenger."

If fear and doubt riddle your project, the first step is to make friends with fear. Fear is not a bad thing. It can be a blessing in disguise if and when it is transformed into positive energy. Dr. Wayne Dyer, in his book *You'll See It When You Believe It*, says "What we don't face we fear and what we fear controls us."

A misconception about fear is that in order to move ahead, one has to completely dispel the fear. If that were the case, one would hardly ever proceed. It's rare that in nonroutine activities, such as those of most projects, we can ever have complete certainty. The idea is to develop courage. Cia Ricco, a body-centered psychotherapist, says "Feel your fears. Acknowledge them." For Cia, being courageous means having the fear and doing it, anyway. In short, "Do it scared."

One of my great fears is public speaking, something I do regularly as part of my job. I do it scared. As part of my mental and emotional preparation, I acknowledge my fear by making a mental movie of the most disastrous speech I could possibly give, including getting booed right off the stage. I then make the opposite movie and get a standing

Fears are not easy for people to face.

ovation. At the very least, the fear is diminished to a point where I can fully function, and feel in control.

For the Project Team

Capitalize on the team members' inevitable fears. Get out your Post-it notes and have them brainstorm all the fears they can think of on the project, both personal and business. Go so far as to ask them what they could do if the mandate were to actually cause the project to fail. Then, use the results as input for risk assessment and to develop the project's critical success factors.

Lesson #4: Choose Your Attitude.   Is the glass half-empty? Half-full? Ask an engineer, and a third response is possible: "Neither. The glass is overdesigned." There is no right answer, and whatever the response, the amount of liquid in the glass remains the same. The response simply depends on your point of view.

A while back, Epictetus from the first century A.D. observed that "People are not disturbed by things, but by the views they take of them." If you own a bird feeder and it has nonfeathered friends for visitors such as squirrels, mice, and the occasional raccoon, you have a choice. Be frustrated by the lack of unwelcome visitors and take preventative measures to discourage them. Or, adopt a new point of view. Think of the bird feeder as an animal feeder. My eight-year-old son exposed me to this breakthrough.

And that can be done by the flick of a mental switch. This truth may be one of the most profound truths impacting the quality of human life. Viktor Frankl, a psychologist and philosopher, discovered the power of choosing one's attitude during his incarceration in a concentration camp during the Holocaust. He and others suffered unconscionable atrocities. In the midst of a misery unfathomable to most of us, Frankl discovered the ultimate freedom.

Here, in a passage from his book *Man's Search for Freedom* (© 1984, Touchstone Books), we are reminded that even though we can't change our circumstances in the short run, we do have control over how we view those circumstances:

> The men walking through the concentration camp may have been few in number, but they offer sufficient proof that everything can be taken from a man but one thing: the last of human freedoms—to choose one's attitude in any given set of circumstances, to choose one's way.

For the Project Team

Often on projects, we are held captive by the negative attitudes and opinions of others who, for any number of reasons, take an adversarial position on our project.

These can be team members, but I am specifically referring to outside stakeholders who will be affected by the project. We ignore their attitudes at our own peril. As projects, both internal and external, impact many constituencies, the ability to effectively manage project influencers is a critical success factor for most projects. An important role of the team leader is to ensure the team has in place a plan to manage project influencers, both friends and foes of the project.

Lesson #5: Stand Up for the Truth.   If I had to pick just one survival skill for project managers and team members, I'd pick the ability to be assertive. By assertive, I mean having the fortitude to tell the truth about a given situation, including the consequences of following a particular request—for example, being told to increase scope without impacting resource requirements or the existing project end date. Being assertive means to be able to say no to unreasonable demands.

You can be a certified project management professional (PMP)® and hold a PhD in project management. But, if you're not assertive, the price of being nice is to do yourself in.

It's a case where a "can-do" attitude is a bad attitude to have. Caving in to unreasonable demands from project sponsors and customers takes its toll on our own self-esteem and puts the project at risk by hiding what's really true. Being a good soldier is irresponsible. And Good Soldier Syndrome is one of the biggest silent killers of projects.

Unless we know how to say "no," call it "nohow," you will find your sense of self-worth eroding, leading you to adopt a victim persona as your primary self-identify.

Here's how to apply "nohow":

- Confirm the request by playing it back in your words.
- Take the time to analyze the impact of the request. Do not respond on the spot.
- Return with fact-based information.
- Have alternatives and make a recommendation.
- Affirm your commitment that you want the project to be a success and are looking out for the best interests of the business.
- Use your judgment to decide to accept the request. If you do, be specific about the potential consequences: "OK. We'll add the feature you requested, with your understanding of its impact on the project schedule, cost, risk, retail pricing of the new running shoe, and the delayed start on the Wizbang project."

Now, ask yourself, what commitments do you presently have on the table that you do not believe are achievable? Are you willing to rene-gotiate these?

For the Project Team

An important role of the team leader is to help the team develop its survival skills, including that of assertiveness. This can be done by en-suring that the team has the requisite infrastructure in place to manage its business. This includes having an agreed-upon process to handle change requests for the project, agreed upon by the sponsor, team members, functional managers, and customers.

Another mechanism that is also effective in enabling the team and the team leader to manage upward is this: Gain agreement on a set of operating norms that the sponsor and functional managers will abide by during the life of the project. For example:

- No changes should be made to team decisions without an explanation.
- Ensure needed resources are made available to fill skill gaps.

Lesson #6: Resolve Conflict.   Conflict can be the lifeblood of a team when the conflict revolves around differing viewpoints on how to solve a problem or how to proceed on the project. Here, conflict is the womb of innovation, giving birth to a solution or concept that no one individual alone might have contemplated. This brand of conflict—call it conflict of ideas—is to be encouraged if we want the best thinking to come forward. But, as Jim Lewis points out in his *Team-Based Project Management* (Amacom, © 1997, pg. 193): "Conflict of ideas may lead to interpersonal conflict, and when this happens, it must be resolved, or damage to the ef-fective functioning of the organization [or team] will result."

Interpersonal conflict between two individuals or among individuals in a group setting can be very difficult to resolve. For instance, as par-ents we often experience a generation gap resulting in conflict over values with our children. Conflict over values is the most difficult of all

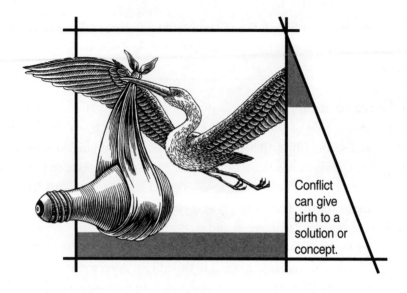

Conflict can give birth to a solution or concept.

to resolve. What do you say and do when your teenage son waltzes into the living room sporting a diamond nose ring?

One-on-One Conflict Resolution

Here are techniques recommended by Jim Lewis. They can be used by a manager with a subordinate, or on a peer-to-peer basis:

- Choose a neutral setting in which to discuss the problem.
- State your sincere desire to resolve the conflict to the satisfaction of both parties.
- Do not assume you know the other person's intentions, thoughts, or feelings.
- Deal with the issues, not the character of the person.
- Where value differences have caused the conflict, deal with the tangible effects of the difference, not the values themselves.
- Practice active listening, rephrasing what the other person has said.
- State what you want as a request, not as a demand.

- Keep in mind that the other person is not bad, mad, or crazy just because you have a difference.
- Try to work on one issue at a time when several exist.
- Don't rush the process.
- Once an agreement is reached, ask the other party if there is anything that might prevent their complying with the agreement.
- Don't make promises you can't keep.
- Always give the person a chance to save face.

Team-based Conflict Resolution

What do you do in a team meeting when Jane and Joe are at each other's throats, where Joe butts in while Jane is interrupting? It's a mistaken notion that the role of the team leader alone is to resolve conflicts in a team setting. On the contrary, it's the job of each and every team member to manage conflict. Two practices that greatly enable team members to manage conflict are to establish team meeting and team operating norms.

Team meeting norms are ground rules created and committed to by the team that govern how members behave during face-to-face or virtual meetings. Meeting norms are developed through brainstorming and consensus. Here are some examples that teams often come up with:

- One person talks at a time.
- Leave rank at the door.
- If you disagree, come up with an alternative.

Team operating norms extend beyond team meetings. These are the ground rules and procedures that address how the team will administer its business and ensure that communication is open, complete, and timely throughout the project. As in the case of meeting norms, team operating norms are developed through brainstorming and consensus. Examples are as follows:

Conflict can be very difficult to resolve.

- Update and communicate the project plan every two weeks.
- Inform others in advance when unable to meet your deadline.
- Ensure the sponsor and functional managers are bought in to team decisions.

Lesson #7: Pull Your Own Strings.   Give yourself permission to be all you can be.

Project managers are on the firing line day in and day out, being continually called upon to make decisions, often on the fly and without clear-cut authority. Being empowered means being self-actualized; that is, being willing to act without having to ask for permission, or without having been given direct authority. In this sense, being empowered means that one's ability to act comes from within and does not require authorization from another. It means developing self-confidence, and it means taking risks.

There are certain decisions we cannot make on our own. For example, I might not be able to authorize a budget increase of $50,000. I need approval. However, the need for permission or authorization can also be a knee-jerk response as well as a cop-out if I fall into the trap of thinking I

Who's pulling your strings?

can't make a move unless I check with the boss. Although it is comforting to know that I have been given the okay, when this becomes my modus operandi, I subtly and effectively relinquish my power. The ultimate payoff for asking too often for permission is that it allows me to always point to someone or someplace else if things don't work out.

But sooner or later it will catch up with me. I'll be held responsible, even though I have subtly given up my responsibility. As the saying goes, "It's easier to ask for forgiveness than permission."

Are you pulling your own strings? If not, who is?

From the wellspring of one's own sense of self-purpose and vision, combined with those same elements for the project, one begins to feel powerful—full of power—from the inside out. Why? Because as the author and psychiatrist Nathaniel Branden reminded us in a seminar I took with him, "No one is coming to the rescue." Except you.

On the Project Team Level

I was recently asked to give a motivational speech to a group of project managers and their team members. Before being introduced, one of the audience members came up to me and said, "I hear you came to motivate us. I'm glad. We could sure use some motivation." I told her that I really can't motivate you. About all I can do is unleash the motivation that's already in you. To allow her to think that I could motivate her would be to take the power from her and put it in my hands. I wanted her to know that she is the source of her own motivation and not to look to me for that. I would be doing her a disservice to have her think otherwise.

The role of the project leader is to co-create with the team an empowering environment, one in which team members participate in making key project decisions, where each member of the core team has an equal opportunity to influence the direction of the project. Establishing team meeting and team operating norms (see lesson #6) are two techniques to set up an empowering environment.

Another technique is to ask individual team members to identify ways in which the purpose of the project connects with their own professional or personal goals.

Lesson #8: Kickback.   Our jobs are demanding, and our to-do lists are endless. And with the help of personal organizers, we are constantly reminded of how much we still have to do, and how far behind we are with our commitments. My Palm Pilot reminds me of this by doing me the favor of displaying all my past-due to-do's in bright red. Are we human beings or are we becoming human doings?

Deepak Chopra, in his audiotape series entitled *Magical Mind, Magical Body*, gives some alarming statistics. He points out that research has discovered we produce an average of 80,000 thoughts per day. Moreover, 90 percent of our thoughts today were the same as the day before. In other words, we are all broken records.

What we need is a vacation. From ourselves. To separate ourselves from our thoughts, just as the clouds are separate from the motionless sky. We need to become the sky, even for a split second. It is in this state of mind (or is it the state of no-mind?) that we open the door to

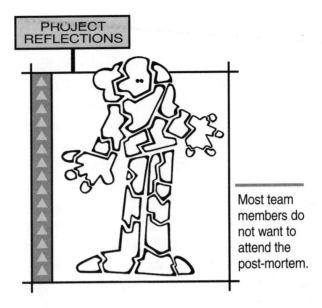

PROJECT
REFLECTIONS

Most team
members do
not want to
attend the
post-mortem.

creativity. New ideas occur in the space between our thoughts. We
have to turn off all the noise.

At the very least, one might invest in a set of relaxation CDs. Or,
take up the practice of meditation.

On the Project Team Level

On projects, reflect kicking back can take the form of looking back on
the project to ferret out lessons learned. Sometimes called the "post-
mortem" session, this is an event that most team members would
rather die than attend. If the project was less than a success, a lot of
scapegoating can go on, and very little is learned. But don't get me
wrong: It's a good idea to do post-project assessments when conducted
in a way where the focus is on what went well, and what you would do
differently, rather than on who messed up.

The very effective team leaders I've seen in action are constantly
taking assessments, especially informal ones, of how the project is doing. In every encounter with team members, the effective team leader

is looking to face the facts every day. She wants to know what's going well and what's not. And she's able to ask in a nonpenalizing way.

Making it safe for team members to speak not only about the good but about the bad and the ugly as well does wonders for keeping a project moving. Not only does it enable constant midcourse corrections, team members are exorcised of their concerns and worries, and are then better able to release and channel their energy in positive ways rather than keep things bottled up out of fear.

Lesson #9: Accept the Unacceptable.   Self-acceptance means making an agreement to not enter into an adversarial relationship with yourself. Examples of not accepting oneself include calling yourself names and putting yourself down. Discounting your accomplishments and not being able to accept praise are also examples of not accepting who you are.

Making a positive change in one's life begins by facing facts and accepting the present situation (and the present "you") rather than arguing with reality. Otherwise, we sink deep into the jungle's quicksand. As a skier, for instance, my complaining about the lack of snow never made it snow. It merely drained my energy and kept me stuck in my present state of anger, unable to move on emotionally. I now strive to always accept a situation over which I can do nothing. But that doesn't mean I like or condone the situation. I just accept it. A key survival skill, then, is to be able to accept the unacceptable. And, if you truly can't accept yourself (or the situation), then practice accepting yourself for not accepting yourself (or the situation). It's magic. Plus, you get to laugh and lighten up when you realize how silly this whole thing is.

For the Project Team

It could be that we are running 20 percent over budget on our project, and are two months behind schedule. Not pretty. No one likes it. But it's a fact, and it's history. Hopefully we've reflected on the situation (lesson #8) and learned from it. Allowing the team to get stuck dwelling on failings and shortcomings saps energy and forward momentum. An important role of a team leader is to help the team to ac-

Taking on the three secrets of the jungle is a daunting task.

cept (not necessarily like) setbacks and mistakes. This means accepting both the facts of the matter as well as how people are feeling about the facts, and doing so without trying to change their feelings. Once the facts and feelings have been aired, you are now in a position to renew the team's energy by choosing where you want to go from here. It's a three-step process: acknowledge, accept, adjust.

Lesson #10: Do Something.

A whole stream of events issues from the decision [to take action], raising in one's favor all manner of unforeseen incidents. And meetings and material assistance, which no man could have dreamt would have come his way.
—*The Scottish Himalayan Expedition*, by W. H. Murray.

Taking on the ten lessons and the three insights of the jungle all at once is a daunting task. You can, however, pick one or two to start with. But start. Any one that strikes you is the place to begin. Listen to your gut.

At the Project Team Level

In working on-site at a client organization every day for three months, I observed one project manager—call him Richard—who spent most of his time staring at his computer screen as he made adjustments to the plan and tracked the project. Day in and day out. To Richard, project management was a spectator sport. The project lived on his boob tube.

Following Richard's logic, we would conclude that a better-looking travel brochure would result in a better vacation. It's tempting to finagle with Microsoft Project and come up with the perfect-looking plan. It can also slow down the project and paint an unrealistic picture of what to expect and when to expect it. Nearperfect planning is not a survival skill. Taking action is.

In many of today's fast-paced project environments, once the goal of the project is initially agreed upon and the direction is set, planning tends to follow action. Act. Plan. Act. Plan. The emphasis is on learning and replanning. Your job is to find the right balance for your particular project. Keep in mind the Japanese saying as a guideline: "Planning without action is a daydream. Action without planning is a nightmare."

The Second Insight: What You See Is What You Get

One Saturday mourning, Jackie, my significant other, and I got up at the crack of dawn to leave for Boston. We were traveling from New York City, where she lived. The main reason I got us up early was to avoid the traffic. To no avail: 4:30 a.m., we're stuck in traffic at a dead standstill on the FDR Drive. Not exhibiting a lot of self-control, I went ballistic beating my fists against the dashboard condemning the mayor, all of New York City, and even the governor for my silly situation. In the middle of my temper tantrum, I noticed that in the car next to ours, there was another couple. They were oblivious to the traffic. In fact, they were kissing passionately. That nearly put me over the edge. Looking at them, I said in a loud voice to myself, "Don't you realize there is traffic out there? How can you be loving it up when we're all stuck in this hell hole?" As if getting crazy about the traffic would get it to actually listen. Then it hit me. I realized we were both in the identical traffic. Yet he was having a good time, and I was miserable. Is it the traffic or is it me? The traffic doesn't care what you want.

You can't change the traffic. About all you can change is your outlook on it. This is not a new idea. The Talmud tells us: "We see things not the way they are. We see things the way we are." Years later, speaking in the 1920s, William James, the preeminent Harvard psychologist, said, "The greatest discovery of our time is that a man can change his reality by changing his thoughts." We are not powerless. How we choose to see things determines our reality.

Taking his idea a step further, Shakti Gawain, in her book *The Path of Transformation* (Nataraj Publishing, © 1993), says, "By making a personal commitment to our own individual transformation process, we begin to change the world around us." Others have summed this up with the refrain "Be the change you want to see."

The failure to grasp this fundamental truth has resulted in senior managers lining the pockets of consultants brought in to implement programs designed to change the organization. If only senior management knew that all they had to do was role-model the practices, behaviors, and values that they would like changed, and others would follow their lead. Change is an inside-out job. So as we thrash around in the project jungle, a good thing to remember is: "It's not the jungle that we conquer, it's ourselves."

The Third Insight: The Universe Is on Your Side

In his book *The Road Less Traveled* (Touchstone Books, © 1978), Scott Peck, starts out by saying, "Life is difficult." This is an undeniable reality for most of us. A logical and natural extension of this experience is that we develop a survival-of-the-fittest mentality, an out-look that sees life as a constant struggle. Something to be conquered. This mind-set, albeit a subtle one for many, puts us squarely in an adversarial relationship with all that is around us, effectively sapping us of vital energy. If this becomes our worldview, we can't win. The universe is too big to take on, and we are destined to a lifelong struggle.

I learned this one time while bowling. Although I am a very occasional bowler—maybe twice a year, if that, when I do play the game—I put a lot of effort and concentration into making a good score. On one memorable evening, while waiting for my turn, I noticed I was seeing the bowling pins as my enemy. My job was to knock them down, and their job was to stay up at all costs. Then the light went on. I said to myself, "Why don't I look at them as being on my side? Wanting to cooperate." I began thinking of them as wanting to fall down as much as I did. I shifted from an adversarial to a harmonious relationship with bowling pins, of all things. That change in outlook alone transformed my game. It improved significantly. Even though I still bowl infrequently, it's not unlikely that I will score anywhere from 145 to 175. Getting two and three strikes in a row is no longer unusual. The lesson: All that changed was my outlook about the world around me to one of being in harmony with my adversaries. The universe wants you to win, and it wants the other guy to win as well.

I later found out that the martial art of aikido is also based on the principle of finding harmony, even when you are in harm's way. Aikido translates as "the way of harmony with the life force," which means uniting our own energy with that of the universe. In his book *Leadership Aikido* (Three Rivers Press, © 1997), John O'Neil sums it up cogently:

Rather than struggle against an opponent, even in the case of an unprovoked dangerous attack, the Aikido master unites himself with the adversaries' energy, by channeling it into harmless directions and avoiding injury to the attacker and defender as well.

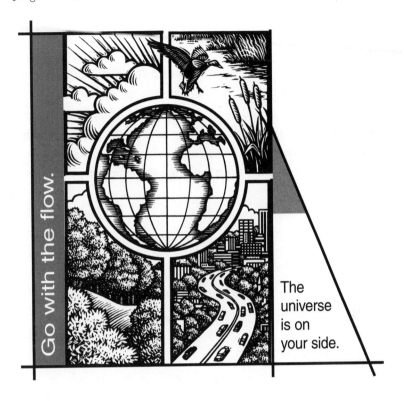

The universe (and the bowling pins) are on our side. All we have to do is choose to see it that way. Then, go with the flow.

Summary

Faced with a continuing stream of new challenges, the twenty-first-century project managers who are effective will need to take the time to focus on the project of all projects . . . the one that stares back at them with hopeful eyes every morning as they look in the mirror to get ready to embark on another day. The silent cry is to master one's own inner game of project management. It means taking steps to start embracing the three insights and applying the ten lessons.

There's good news: To put these insights and lessons into action, you don't have to wait for anything or anyone outside of you to do anything. You can start right now, even before you read the next sentence. Or not. That's because nobody is coming to the rescue—which is also good news, because you don't have to depend on anybody else to get started. It will be up to each of us to take responsibility, to respond with ability (or disability). It's a choice. Because in the project jungle of the twenty-first century, there will be no victims, only volunteers.

chapter 8

How Do I Get There?—
Taking Charge of Your Own Career

Introduction

You have answered the questions "Where am I?" and "Where do I want to go?" The final question is, "How do I get there?" That is the topic of this chapter. Let's take an inventory of exactly what you have accomplished so far. First, you have profiled your skills and compared the profile with each of the four types of project managers. From that analysis you know where you are with respect to the required skill profile for each project manager type. Second, you have also explored possible futures with respect to project management. You know whether you will be an occasional or dedicated project manager and where you would like to be relative to the career ladder for project managers and beyond. In this chapter we will develop a strategy and action plan for you that will help you realize your project manager career goal.

> . . . if you don't know where you are going, how will you know when you get there?

Developing a Professional Development Plan

The foundation of your professional development plan (PDP) will be your vision and mission statements. Simply put, if you don't

Take charge of your own career.

know where you are going, how will you know when you get there? Or, as Alice in Wonderland discovered, If you don't know where you are going, any road will get you there. We would like to think that you intend to be a little more purposeful than Alice!

The first thing we want to do is document the decisions you have made relative to your future as a project manager. This document will contain your personal vision and mission statements and your tactical plan for achieving your mission. The first two are not lengthy statements, but they are still difficult to write. We will help you with them by way of examples, using Bob Wysocki's PDP. The vision statement and the mission statement are usually one or two sentences that talk about who you want to be and how others will recognize you. So let's take a closer look at each of these statements.

The Vision Statement

This is a statement of an ideal end state that you would like to attain. It is not likely to change. Since it is ideal, it is something you will strive for all of your professional career. You may not ever get there but you will always be

> **This is a statement of an ideal end state that you would like to attain . . . it is something to be pursued.**

working toward that goal. In other words, you know where you are headed—at least in general terms. Figure 8.1 is the vision statement from Bob Wysocki's PDP.

Note that Bob's vision statement is stated in such a fashion that he will always be working toward it. That is, it is something to be pursued. It is not formulated in a way that Bob can ever really say it has been achieved, but at the same time it does give Bob a sense of direction. For every action that he might contemplate doing, he can evaluate whether or not it contributes to his vision. If it doesn't, the next question is, "Why do it?" There may be compelling reasons or extenuating circumstances that lead him to do it, but it will be done with the full knowledge that it may not contribute to the attainment of his vision.

Before you go any further, try your hand at writing your own personal vision statement. This is not something you need to share with

---

VISION STATEMENT

To be recognized as having made a valued and lasting contribution to the practice of project managment.

FIGURE 8.1   An Example of a Vision Statement

anyone except your most trusted mentor or significant other, so be open and honest about recording your innermost desires.

The Mission Statement

Your mission statement is a realization of your vision statement. It is a more specific statement about how others will see you in the context of your project manager development. It is a statement of what you will be doing. In other words, it is something to be accomplished. It can have multiple parts and may be modified over time. The changes are likely to be additions or revisions to earlier mission statements. The changes could represent a radical shift in focus, though this is not likely to be the case. Figure 8.2 is the mission statement from Bob Wysocki's PDP.

> **It is a statement of what you will be doing . . . it is something to be accomplished.**

Note that Bob's mission statement is an instantiation of his vision statement. It is a concrete action statement, and progress towards it can be measured. This is not necessarily the case with the vision statement.

> **It is a concrete action statement, and progress toward it can be measured.**

Now take your vision statement and translate it into your mission statement. Don't be too

---

MISSION STATEMENT

To develop and implement a comprehensive portfolio of assessment tools to help organizations increase the success rate of their projects.

FIGURE 8.2 An Example of a Mission Statement

narrowly focused or short-term in your thinking. This is still a long-range statement.

Tactical Plans

This is where the rubber meets the road, and you will get very specific about what you intend to do to realize your mission. Depending on how detailed you wish to plan, you may want to include completion dates in your tactical plans. We choose not to, and for good reason. Our tactical plan is a list of all those things we would like to do to move ahead in our professional development. You may not be able to control many of them and merely list them so that if the opportunity presents itself you will take advantage of it. This list will change quite frequently as activities are completed and new ones are identified. Remember, you are smarter tomorrow than you are today. You will learn about new opportunities and associated activities to add that are within the scope of your mission statement. Figure 8.3 is that tactical plan from Bob Wysocki's PDP.

> . . . a list of all those things we would like to do to move ahead in our professional development.

Note that every specific activity in Bob's tactical plan contributes to his mission statement—some more than others. In the example given here, every action item relates to a single-part mission statement. In a more general situation, the mission statement can be a multipart statement. In that case, every tactical action must relate to at least one part of your mission statement. The more parts that it relates to, the more important that action item will be to your achieving your vision statement.

Now it's your turn. Take your mission statement and list all of those things you would like to do to realize your mission. Even though it may not be obvious to you at this time how you will do these things, list them. You don't want to miss any opportunity that comes along. Our

---

TACTICAL PLAN

Identify and integrate into the EII portfolio existing tools that can be used to improve the practice of project management with special emphasis on team effectiveness.

Annually deliver a minimum of four public presentations on improving project team effectiveness.

Establish partnerships with companies that provide tools that can be adapted to the improvement of project team effectiveness.

Discover areas of need for team effectiveness tools. Develop and implement tools to meet those needs.

Provide web access to the EII portfolio.

Develop and deliver team effectiveness and related project management web based training modules.

FIGURE 8.3 An Example of a Tactical Plan

caveat is, if it isn't in your plan, it isn't going to happen. Err on the side of putting too much into your tactical plan. Here are some further guidelines for you to consider as you begin to develop your tactical plan.

On-the-Project Training. Being sent away for training is a rare event for many of us. What do you do if you are numbered among the training deprived and have a need to improve certain of your project management skills? We all want to grow up to be world class project managers, and training is an integral part of achieving this goal. Maybe some of you simply don't have the opportunity or time for the formal training you need and deserve. Take heart. All is not lost. We have some suggestions for you.

We don't know what your organization looks like as far as project management practices are concerned, but let's assume there are project

We all want to grow up to be a world-class project manager.

managers who know more than you do about managing projects or who have the project management skills you want to improve upon. Even if there are only a few of them, you need to find a way to get into their heads and learn what they know about project management. You might wonder, "How is this possible? They are so busy putting out fires, they don't have any time for me." Well, for starters, you should do everything you could to get assigned to their projects.

For example, let's say that Chris Tullball is one of the best project planners to ever pass through the portals **Get involved** of your company. You have read about planning, but somehow nothing translates into practice. Obviously planning is a skill you need to develop further. Get on Chris's team, or at least offer to help her with the upcoming planning session she is running. Be her gofer, make copies, get coffee. Do anything you can to take part in the planning process. Your agenda is to get some practical ideas from Chris by watching her in action. She won't refuse your honest offer of help.

So you are already a great planner. Identify some other skill that needs development. Find someone who is very good at practicing that skill. Get involved with them. Put yourself in a situation where you can observe an expert practicing the skill you need to develop. You will be doing real work (something the project manager will get value from), and you will be developing your skills at the same time (something you will get value from).

Marketing Yourself for Career Development.   Have you ever given any thought to how you might use your work situation to promote yourself and grow your career as a project manager? Probably not. We would like to offer a few suggestions as to what you might want to do to promote yourself. We're not talking about bragging or self-serving proclamations, but rather about a sound strategy for professional development.

Tell your manager about your career goals. If your manager doesn't know what you want to be when you grow up, how can he or she be expected to help you get there? We've seen numerous examples of professional staff who keep their goals a secret. Somehow they have the notion that their manager might think they are not happy with their present situation and are looking for

> # Give your manager a chance to help you . . .

something else to do. Others might think that by helping them, their manager risks losing them to some other department or company. Remember that *you* are in charge of your career, not your manager. Give your manager a chance to help you through work assignments and training. If they aren't predisposed to help you, you might want to give serious thought to finding another manager and another job.

Make sure senior project managers know about your development interests. This one is so important to your future that we want you to pay close attention to what we have to offer by way of a strategy that we know works. We've been there and done that. You know what skills and competencies you need to further develop. Make sure other pro-

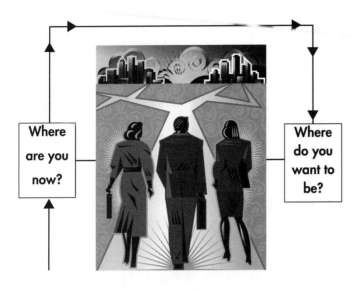

ject managers know this, too, and volunteer to help out on projects where there will be an opportunity to get some good OJT. If you want to be a little more proactive, seek out projects where those development opportunities will present themselves.

Seek out the WOW Projects. For the serious student of project management, this is a must read. We won't repeat what he had to say. We'll leave it to you to study his article and follow the advice he gives.

Uncovering the Hidden Development Gems in Projects. By now you should have a career development plan in place. It should answer the following two questions: Where are you now? and Where do you want to go? Where are you now is nothing more than a profile of what you do and what you know. What you know is a skill profile that identifies your skill level for skills in the project management, general management, business, personal, and interpersonal areas. Where you want to go is a description of your current career goal as best you can describe it as well as the skill profile of that career goal. In a previous section we

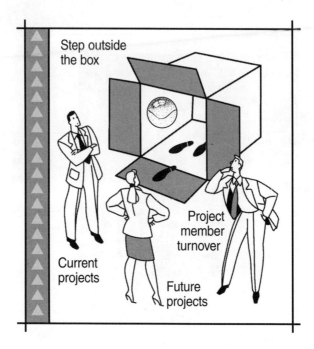

talked about the gap between these two skill profiles. In this section we consider closing the gap with on-the-job training through projects.

The first thing we want to do is assess the OJT opportunities that your company's project portfolio presents to you. This will require some detective work on your part and then the courage to step outside the box. There are three places to look: current projects, future projects, and project team member turnover.

Current project opportunities. From among the current project portfolio, find out what these projects are about and which ones may provide OJT opportunities for you. Get to know someone on the project team and get them to talk to you about how things are going, what problems the team is facing, and how they are doing with respect to the deliverables schedule. If the project has needs that you can contribute and through your contribution you will further develop needed skills, you may want to talk with the project manager.

Future project opportunities. From among the future projects (even those not yet planned or approved), find out what these projects are about and what team skills will be needed. Again, are there opportunities for you to contribute and learn as a result? If so, you will want to talk with the project manager.

Staff turnover opportunities. Finally, the real hidden gem may surface as a result of staff turnover. When a team member leaves for whatever reason, there is a need that must be filled. If your filling it will put you in a position to further your development needs, talk to the project manager.

Once you have identified these opportunities, you will need to muster the courage to step outside the box. That is, you have to take the initiative and push the boundaries of your job in those directions. This may mean an added workload, but if you want to get ahead, this is the way to do it. So swallow hard and get on with your future. We have said it before and we say it again: Your company owns your job, but you own your career.

I Have My PDP—Now What?   Congratulations. You now have a document that defines where you are going and how you are going to get there. This is an important milestone in your professional development, and you should be proud of the work you have done so far. You have a tool that will allow you to move forward with confidence. There are a few things we would like to tell you about how to proceed from here.

The PDP Is Dynamic

What we mean here is that your PDP will be in a constant state of flux. As you make progress toward an intermediate goal, you will stop and reevaluate. The result may be a revision of your plan. That's normal. The PDP isn't written to be put on the shelf and forgotten. It is a living document that you should always

> **. . . your PDP will be in a constant state of flux.**

have in mind as you encounter new opportunities for professional activity. Always evaluate them in the face of your plan. Do they fit? If not, do they suggest a change in plans? If they do, should they be done now or postponed? If postponed, will the chance to take advantage of them come again?

The PDP Should Be Shared

Don't keep it a secret, but don't post it on your web page, either. Share your PDP with your line manager, with your mentor, with the director of your project office, with the training department, and with the human resources department. All of them can be helpful in locating opportunities that will further your plan. They have to know about it to help you, though.

The PDP Should Be Posted

To make sure that you are always aware of your PDP, we advise you to post it in your cubicle. Put it somewhere where you can see it, and it will always be a reminder to you to look for those development opportunities. If it is out of sight, it may be out of mind. Don't take that risk. It is too important to your future.

Mentors

One of the most often overlooked resources is the mentor. They are all around you, and you work with them every day. They might hold the next position for which you are preparing yourself. They might simply possess a skill you are trying to acquire. In any case, they have achieved something to which you aspire, and their advice and counsel is available and free for the asking. Some of you may be fortunate to work for a company that has a formal mentoring program, but we do not believe that is necessary. In this section we explore who these mentors are,

> **. . . they have achieved something to which you aspire, and their advice and counsel is available and free for the asking.**

what they do, and how you can take advantage of their availability to help your career.

What Is a Mentor?

The *American Heritage Dictionary* defines a mentor as a wise and trusted counselor or teacher. A mentor is an individual you might look to for help or advice on any aspect of your personal or professional life. In the context of your professional growth and development as a project manager, a mentor will most likely be a fellow project management professional. He or she might hold a position that you aspire to or they might possess a skill that you would like to master. As you develop as a project management professional, you will most likely change mentors and in fact might have more than one mentor at a time.

> **As you develop as a project management professional, you will most likely change mentors and in fact might have more than one mentor at a time.**

To be an effective mentor does not require extensive skills in counseling or psychology. Rather, it requires an attitude that is supportive and directive. Good human relations skills are the foundation for successful mentoring. These include interpersonal skills (being approachable, collaborative, a conflict manager, and a decision maker), communications skills (active listener, gives feedback, and is a good speaker), and leadership skills (motivates, is open, and is supportive of change).

Mentors are typically older than their mentorees (or mentees, if you prefer) but not that much older. The mentor will have been there and done that, so they can impart their experience and on-the-job wisdom to their mentorees. If they are too much older, there may be a generation gap to deal with.

Find
yourself
a mentor.

What Does a Mentor Do?

As we have said, a mentor is first and foremost a good listener. He or
she is your safe harbor, and a person whom you should be able to take
into your confidence with your most sensitive issues and concerns. To
be specific, a mentor might

1. Help you formulate a career plan.
2. Help you examine alternatives and make a decision.
3. Identify resources inside or outside of the organization.
4. Point you to others with more in-depth knowledge or
    experience in a specific area.
5. Create networking opportunities for you.
6. Introduce you to the right people.

7. Share their experiences.
8. Be safe harbor to you.
9. Act as your confidante.
10. Be ready to listen when you just need to talk to someone.

Find Yourself a Mentor

We all have mentors, whether they are recognized formally or informally. Surely there are people in your life whom you admire and try to emulate. If you simply let these people influence your life, you have informal mentors. If you go one step further and ask their advice and for them to share their wisdom with you, you have formal mentors.

The extent to which a mentor works with you can vary. For example, if you want to be the best senior project manager in your company, find someone who already is and build a relationship with them, and sooner or later you will feel comfortable asking them to be your mentor. Or, let's suppose you are having trouble honing

> **PMI™ has an extensive local chapter network. Get involved!**

your project planning skills. Find someone in your organization who is a recognized project planning expert, get to know them, help them with their planning sessions, and sooner or later you will feel comfortable asking them to be your planning mentor.

What if your company doesn't have such project managers? You will need to look outside. Here is where your professional involvement in the Project Management Institute can be helpful. PMI™ has an extensive local chapter network. Get involved! Conference attendance can lead to professional relationships and, in time, to mentors as well.

Benefits to Mentor and Mentoree

For the mentor, the benefits are psychological and personal. The psychological rewards come from having helped someone acquire skills and achieve their goals. The personal rewards are the self-esteem and job satisfaction that come from having someone think enough of you to ask you to work with them in this closely guarded personal relationship.

For the mentoree, there are a number of benefits. First will be the added knowledge and productivity gains that will obviously result. Just having someone who will listen and offer advice to solve problems and give you an unbiased opinion on issues important to you is value enough.

Managing Politics in Projects

There are a lot of people who find organizational politics very distasteful. No doubt we have all seen someone who has run roughshod over others to advance himself in the organization. This kind of backstabbing politics is definitely despicable, and we certainly don't advocate that you practice such behavior.

> **... all behavior in an organization is a political act!**

However, we can't escape the fact that all behavior in an organization is a political act! You are always under scrutiny from others, and you are always influencing others, whether you intend to or not. In fact, you can't *not* be of influence! Even silence can influence. When you sit beside someone on a plane and read or look out the window, and give them very short responses to their attempts to communicate with you, they usually get the message: I don't want to enter into a relationship with you.

So you can't avoid influencing others, even if you want to, and you can't therefore avoid being political. The answer is to understand politics and make your behavior as positive as possible.

> **... the purpose of all political behavior is to gain and keep power or control.**

First, understand that the purpose of all political behavior is to gain and keep power or control. Furthermore, you must recognize that if you are a project manager, you must have some power, or else you cannot get the job done successfully. One of the most common complaints of project managers is that they have a lot of responsibility but no authority. What they mean is that they have no position power, which is conferred on individuals by organizations. Project managers are often second-class citizens in the overall scheme of organizational hierarchies. And when they are in a matrix organization, in which they must get all of their resources from functional departments, they find that the functional managers regard them as a nuisance. Furthermore, the functional manager is rewarded for getting functional work done, rather than for supporting projects, which is something that needs to be changed if an organization is to be really effective in managing projects.

One suggestion: It is your relationship with the functional manager that makes all the difference in the world when you need resources. The most effective project managers are those who take time to build a network of relationships with other members of the organization, and building these relationships is a political act. If you don't have the inclination to do this, then you are missing the most important opportunity available to you to advance your project management career.

Does this mean go out drinking beer with them, or socializing with them off the job? Not necessarily, although a limited amount of such activity would help. But you do need to get to know them, find out what their interests are, what makes them tick. Then, when you need help from them, they are more willing to give it. On the other hand, if you are a nameless face in the organization, you may find them very uncooperative.

Another aspect of politics and power that you should know about is the principle of reciprocity. This is commonly referred to as "you owe me one," because the other person has done you a favor. When done in a cold, callous, calculating way, it is an obnoxious practice, but there is no doubt that we feel obligated to return legitimate favors that someone else has done for us. This means that you should never refuse a request for help from someone else if you can possibly accommodate them, because you may need to "call in" that favor at some later time. In addition, when you help others, you are judged to be a cooperative person with whom they can work, and this is always a bonus for you.

What's in It for Me?

One of the most important principles of psychology is the WIIFM rule—people only do something if there is something in it for themselves. Yes, this even includes benevolent acts. The person gets a feeling of having done something good. If he doesn't, then he isn't likely to do anything benevolent.

> **People only do something if there is something in it for themselves.**

You should remember this rule and apply it to your projects. What it means is that you must try to help members of the team get something that they value from their participation. If there is nothing in it for them, then you can't expect them to be very motivated to do the work you need done.

How to Influence Without Direct Authority

Notice that all of what we have said is aimed at exerting influence when you have no direct authority. Also be aware that, even when you have direct authority, you still need to exercise influence. The use of direct authority can be thought of as using position power or coercive power over others. Coercive power means you force someone to do something, and this kind of power is very unlikely to work in any organization today.

But even position power is highly overrated. We have interviewed a number of CEOs and asked them these questions:

- "You have a lot of authority in the organization, right?" They agree that they do.
- "Does your authority guarantee that people will do what you want done?" They always say, "Of course not."
- "Then how do you get people to do what must be done?" we ask.

They have all told us that they must get the person to want to do it. The only thing the authority allows them to do is exercise sanctions

You need to exercise influence even without direct authority

over the person if he or she doesn't comply, and these sanctions are limited by the law and by how much time the executive can spend dealing with the situation. So in the end, even the CEO has to use influence to get things done.

You and I can hope to do no better.

Sharpen your skills at communicating, negotiating, building relationships, and influencing. They are all political behaviors, and you are going to need them to be successful in your career!

Summary

You have finally reached the end. We hope the product you have developed meets your expectations. You have a plan and a way to make it happen. Think of it as a start. As each day passes and as each experience mounts, you will want to revisit your plan. It will change. Expect that. To have it otherwise would be to have nothing more than fish wrapping.

You might want to share the last chapter with your manager and anyone else in a position to make the environment a little more supportive. There is a lot of advice in the last chapter that may help.

chapter 9

Organizational Support

Introduction

This book would not be complete without a chapter that deals with how the enterprise can facilitate the career development of world class project managers. So this chapter is for senior managers, managers of project managers, human resource development specialists, and anyone else involved in the care and feeding of fledgling project managers.

Firing Begins with Hiring

As we have written earlier, many project managers didn't choose project management as a career; they had the job thrust upon them. And in some cases, this is because the organization has no separate career path for project managers and technical people. If you want to advance in your career as a technical person, you do so by becoming a project manager.

The result is often tragic. You lose a good technical person over time because it is almost impossible to maintain a high level of technical skills and also be a manager. And you also find that many of these technical specialists make poor project managers because they lack the people skills that are so vital to doing the job well.

The first thing you should consider is that selecting people who have the desire and aptitude for the job is critical to the ultimate suc-

You can
lose good
people
over time

cess of that individual in the job. Just because a person is good at his or
her technical job does not mean that he or she will make a good project manager. In fact, if she is exceptionally good at technical work, she

will probably *not* make a
good project manager, one
reason being she will find it
hard to manage the project
without meddling in the
technical work.

> **Just because a person is good at his or her technical job does not mean that he/she will make a good project manager.**

The message is: If you select for the job a person who
is unsuited for it, you will just have to replace that individual later on, so
you have done him or her a great disservice in placing him in the job.

As we have tried to show, not everyone is cut out to be a project
manager, any more than everyone is cut out to be a butcher, baker, or
candlestick maker. To each of us is given certain aptitudes, and rather
than try to force the square peg into a round hole, it is far better to find
a round peg in the first place.

In the chapter on profiles of project managers, we have shown the kind of attributes that make good project managers. Use these as guidelines in selecting people for the job. Then go the next step and give them the support they need to really make it.

How to Support the Developing Project Manager

Aptitude is the starting point, but aptitude must be turned into skill. We can learn a good lesson from sports. A coach finds a person who seems to have a real aptitude for a sport. Does the coach put the player on the team and say, "Go play ball?" No. He nurtures the natural talent of the rookie. He teaches him how to use his skills to advantage, to get progressively better. By the time a player becomes a star, his former coaches have invested an enormous amount of time in nurturing that talent, training, practicing, rehearsing. Nobody is *born* a superstar.

We seem to be totally unaware of this in organizations. We use the *shark-bait* approach to dealing with people in the work place. We throw a person into a job with no concern for whether they have aptitude, then give them no help, let the sharks eat them up, then fire them when they don't perform.

We talk about human resource *development,* but seldom is true HRD applied to anyone other than rising superstars who are on a fast track to the top of the organization. We need to do the same for other members of the enterprise—especially project managers.

Assign a mentor to help guide them.

Encourage fledgling project managers to treat their job as a true career path, not as an accidental job. Suggest that they join the Project Management Institute and attend regular chapter meetings so they can network with other members of the profession. Assign a mentor to help guide them. Encourage them to hang in there when the going gets rough, because it will get rough on some projects.

Start them with small jobs and gradually increase their responsibilities until they can handle the really big jobs.

Above all, make sure they get the training they need in the project management body of knowledge, which we have discussed in an earlier chapter of this book. One way to do this is to enroll them in certificate programs offered by universities and

> **. . . make sure they get the training they need . . .**

other providers around the country. Have them become project management professionals (PMP®). Or, if the person is really serious and excited about project management as a profession, encourage him or her to get a master's degree in project management. This is equivalent to an MBA, but with project management as the primary focus.

The Position Itself

Another thing that is important is to give the position some standing in the organization. For a very long time, functional managers have been "king," and project management has been a stepchild that many of those managers resented. In their book *Creating an Environment for Successful Projects* (Jossey-Bass Publishers, © 1997), Robert J. Graham and Randall L. Englund suggest that organizations should view functional groups as being there to serve the needs of projects. In doing so, project managers are elevated to the same status in the enterprise as that of functional managers, if not slightly higher. Only in this manner can project managers get the level of support from functions that they really need to meet critical project targets.

The position of project manager should also have the standing of other positions by giving it a proper job description, pay scale, and so on. Further, the organization should establish a true dual career path, in which technical personnel can advance up a technical ladder and make as much money as members of the management staff. By doing this, they are less tempted to become managers when their true love is technical work. In addition, those individuals who really want to manage projects can do so and hone their skills to perfection.

Actually, there is good reason to suggest that perhaps the ladder should have three branches rather than two. There is definitely a dif-

Establish a true dual-career path.

ference between managing projects and managing a department. Since the project manager frequently has people assigned to her team by functional managers, so that she has a lot of responsibility and no authority, she needs a slightly different set of skills compared with those of the department manager. She has to worry less about performance appraisals and daily administrative duties, but she has to have exceptional political skills—something that is not quite as critical to the functional manager.

We believe, in fact, that the role of project manager will eventually become the stepping-stone for high-level CEOs, because project managers usually have to interact with people from nearly every department in the organization, as well as people outside. We also believe that, like CEOs, the project manager who has a balanced HBDI profile will have the advantage of being able to interface with people who have any and all thinking preferences, because she can communicate well with them and translate between the different quadrants.

This should not be misunderstood, however. We are not suggesting that *only* individuals with balanced profiles be selected as project managers. For one thing, only about 2 percent of the population have such profiles, so you won't find many candidates who match the requirement. But most importantly, we have shown that people of all profiles can be good project managers if they are willing to augment their least-preferred thinking styles with extra effort or support from team members who have those preferences.

The Project Office

To some managers, the term "project office" conveys the idea of bureaucracy and attendant red tape. So if you don't like this term, call it a "project management function," because that is what it is, and we believe from our experience that there is great merit in organizing this way. As we have shown, not everyone is cut out to be a project manager, so having a function staffed by dedicated project managers has a number of advantages. Some of these are discussed as follows:

The project manager can hone his or her skills because that is the entire function to be performed. He or she can develop both breadth and depth in project management skills. She is freed from the temptation to do both managing and doing. Her role is to manage the project, not to do technical work. This frees the technical people from the "burden" of doing project administrative work, which many of them hate doing, and allows them to develop their technical competencies in the same way that project managers develop theirs.

Ultimately, the project office should employ a full-time scheduler if there are four or more project managers. This person can be a clerical-level person, who can free project managers to do management rather than sit in front of a computer several days a week massaging their schedules. We have worked with several companies that have done this and realized significant cost savings. A fringe benefit is that the clerical person gets to do something more challenging than routine clerical duties. This truly puts the project manager on an equal footing with

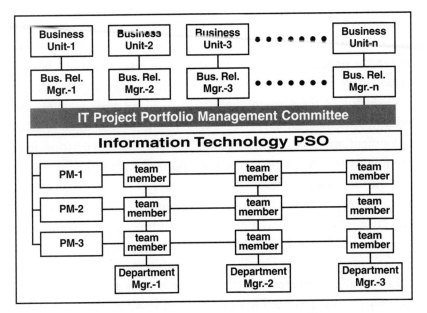

FIGURE 9.1   An Information Technology Project Support Office

other functional managers, since the project office is now viewed as a function in its own right.

The office serves as the focal point for the entire organization. It is now easier to achieve alignment of projects with overall enterprise strategy, because fewer project managers can become more closely aligned with that strategy than is possible when everyone is trying to manage projects. Does this setup mean that other members of the organization need know nothing about project management? Not at all. One of the core principles of good project management is that the people who must do project work should participate in developing the project plan. So everyone needs some understanding of project management.

Figure 9.1 displays a typical organizational structure and placement of a project support office. We include it here because it will be instructive to identify the players and how they can be of help to you in your professional development.

Let's take a closer look at who those players are and how they can be of help. Let's start at the top. Business relationship managers are the link between the project support office and the business units. Each business unit will have at least one such person, and they will have firsthand knowledge of all the projects that are planned for their business unit. Find out what those projects entail and whether any of them offer you development opportunities. If so, you will want to take a personal interest in following them along the path to approval and putting in your bid to get on those project teams. The next player of interest to you will be the project support office manager. They should have an enterprise-wide perspective on projects that are nearing the proposal stage or that have staffing needs. While this is a little further along in the project life cycle than the knowledge that a business relationship manager will have, they are still valuable to you for exactly the same reasons as the business relationship manager. You need to be on the inside with all of these people. The other two positions of interest will be the current project managers and the resource managers. We have talked about your relationship with them in Chapter Six and will not repeat that here. And so you can see how the project support office offers a number of opportunities. All you have to do is pay attention and position yourself to seize the day!

Executive Briefings

This raises an important issue. We find many enterprises that spend significant amounts of money training people in project management without realizing the expected gains from their investment. The reason is that middle and senior managers do not understand what project management is.

The common misconception is that project management is just scheduling. Jim Lewis even found this in Germany. A manager in a German company told him that he was trying to explain to senior managers what project management is, and one of them said, "I don't understand why we don't just buy Microsoft Project and do it [meaning project management]." Jim assured him that this same belief is alive and well in the United States.

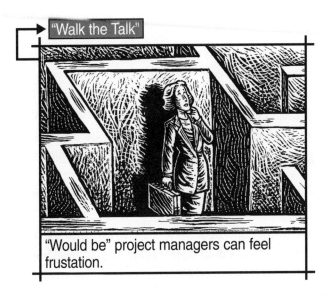

"Walk the Talk"

"Would be" project managers can feel frustation.

The reason for this is simple: Until recent years, business schools did not deal with project management. It was not recognized as a specialized discipline, so many senior managers have had no formal education in what it is all about, and they have unrealistic expectations about what project managers can achieve.

As an example of this, a fellow who attended Jim's class on project management told him that when he returned to work, he got his team into the conference room and started developing a plan for his project. His boss came by, saw them in the meeting, and called the project manager outside. "What are you doing?" he asked.

"Developing a project plan," said the project manager.

"You don't have time for that," snapped his boss. "Get them out of the conference room so they can get the job done."

And this attitude is more prevalent than you may think. To a great extent, we pay lip service to planning, but most of us don't "walk the talk." This leaves would-be project managers feeling frustrated and unappreciated. More importantly, they are paralyzed and ineffective as a result.

If, as Tom Peters contends, project management is a core competency without which organizations cannot survive in this new millennium, then we need to develop a better understanding and appreciation for what it is all about and support it in the same way that we would support any core competency.

> **. . . project management is a core competency . . .**

Further, as we have mentioned, projects must be aligned with business strategy. This is commonly referred to as project portfolio management. The enterprise has a portfolio of projects that are key to its overall business strategy. These have been carefully selected and are managed by project managers who have the skills needed for success.

Change Your Accounting Procedures

Organizations that have not had strong project management typically budget only departments, and projects are just accidental to how they do work. This is unacceptable if you want to really manage projects correctly.

A project must have its own budget. It is indeed a paper transfer within the organization when the project is strictly internal, but it is a major element of proper project control.

> **A project must have its own budget.**

What we are saying is that people from functional groups who are assigned to the project have their time charged to the project, which goes back to their departments as a budget credit. This is one way to make everyone aware of what a project really costs, and keeps functional managers from jealously guarding the time of their people because they don't want to spend money from their own budgets unwisely.

You also must have a proper project information system, which means that time spent on the project is charged to the job, not to the functional department, and the same for other expenses.

- You should have a project review board that is responsible for approving changes to project plans.
- You must have a proper project selection process, so that projects don't just ooze up out of the mud without having business merit.
- You should also have a project cancellation process that kills projects that have become losers.

You must allow project managers to have input to the performance appraisals of team members. They would not appraise the technical performance of those people, but rather evaluate such factors as cooperativeness, communication, timeliness of work, commitment to the project, and so on. Only by having such input can a project manager hope to have commitment and loyalty to the project.

Changing the Organizational Culture

When you have been running projects for years in a totally unstructured way and you decide to adopt a structured approach, this is a major change in culture. Any senior manager who has ever tried to change the organization's culture knows that it is not easy. People who are SJ temperaments are motivated to maintain stability and order, and these individuals often occupy many of the middle management positions in any company. So the very change that the senior executive wants to make may be unconsciously resisted by the very people who must help make it happen.

Experience has shown that it takes from two to five years for an organization to reach maturity in project management. There are about five levels of maturity, and it often takes a year per stage.

Dr. Harold Kerzner wrote a book entitled *In Search of Excellence in Project Management* (Van Nostrand Reinhold, © 1998), in which he reported his findings in a survey of approximately 250 organizations, out of which only thirty-nine met his criteria for excellence in project management. No doubt if he had been able to survey the thousands of organizations nationwide that are trying to make project management work, he would have found a much smaller percentage of excellent organizations.

It takes time to achieve results.

Knowing that it takes time to achieve results is helpful, because when we engage in some change effort, thinking we will achieve quick results, and find that this is not happening, it is easy to lose patience and give up the effort. This is part of what happened with the quality circle movement, the self-directed work team movement, and other programs that promised great rewards. The companies that stayed with these programs usually got results, but many other organizations abandoned them after a brief foray, because results were not quickly forthcoming.

There has been much written about organizational change, and one premise is that a "burning platform" issue is needed to provoke such change and make it "take." The term comes from an incident that happened on a North Sea oil platform. They had a fire, and one individual jumped several hundred feet into the frigid water of the North Sea. The prevailing wisdom is that you can only survive in that temperature

for about fifteen minutes, so jumping in is not usually the best thing to do.

When asked why he had jumped, anyway, the man said, "It was certain I would be fried if I stayed on the platform. I figured I may as well take my chances in the water."

So with many organizations. Unless the platform is burning and there is no other hope for survival, they won't engage in the real change that is needed. They will try various patches, which usually only attack symptoms, while leaving underlying problems unsolved.

If your organization is experiencing a burning platform issue, you can expect that many people are ready for change and may well embrace it. But do you have to wait until the situation is so critical to initiate change?

Not according to John McDonald (1998). He says there are two kinds of responses to our environment that organizations can make. One is revolutionary change, which is typified by the burning platform issue. The other is evolutionary change, in which everyone recognizes that the situation is not critical but that it will become so if change is not made. It is usually much less costly, less traumatic, and much smoother to engage in evolutionary change, so we would urge senior managers to try to initiate this kind of change program rather than wait until the platform is on fire.

Change the Reward System

There is a tenet of organizations that says, "What is rewarded gets done." Everyone is inclined to maximize those measures that are used to assess their performance and that may be used to dispense rewards. For example, you cannot reward competition and expect cooperation. You cannot measure functional managers on how well their departments perform and expect them to willingly give resources to projects when doing so will hurt their department performance.

> **What is rewarded gets done.**

Ask yourself: what behavior do we want to encourage? Then set up reward systems that will get the desired result. And be careful of concluding that you must have incentive pay systems in place. The most powerful rewards are intangibles—a pat on the back from one's boss, recognition and admiration from one's peers, and the fun and challenge of doing the work itself. Consider these and how they currently work, and make whatever changes are needed to get the results you want.

> **What behavior do we want to encourage?**

Walk the Talk

One given is that good projects require teamwork, and teamwork means that people work in a cooperative manner. If the senior management team does not work as a team, if they engage in political backstabbing, then employees at lower levels will not work as teams, either. You have to walk the talk. Lead by example. So you must begin with yourselves, make necessary changes, and then you can ask for those changes in others.

Summary

You can't just train project managers and expect that project management will become a way of life next week. Nor can you buy everyone a copy of a scheduling software package and hope that it will make instant project managers of them. There is no instant pudding recipe for making project management work. It takes hard work, and must be both supported and driven by senior management.

Resources for
Project Managers

Professional Associations

Following is a listing of some of the professional associations that may be of interest to project managers. Information is provided on how to contact them, but with no endorsement as to whether they are worthwhile.

Project Management Institute

Four Campus Boulevard
Newtown Square, PA 19073–3299
Tel: 610–356–4600
FAX: 610–356–4647
www.pmi.org

PMI has local chapters throughout the United States. Contact the main number listed above for information on who to contact in your area if you are interested in a chapter.

Internet

Secretariat
Internet/CRB Switzerland
Zentralstrasse 153
Zurick CH 8003 Switzerland

American Management Association

1601 Broadway
New York, NY 10019

Tel: 212–586–8100
www.amanet.org

Institute of Electrical and Electronic Engineers

345 E. 47th Street
New York, NY 10017–2366
Tel: 212–705–7900
www.ieee.org

National Management Association

2210 Arbor Blvd.
Dayton, OH 45439–1580
Tel: 513–294–0421

American Society for Training and Development

1630 Duke Street
Alexandria, VA 22313
Tel: 703–683–8100

Magazines, Journals, and Newsletters

Following is a listing of several trade magazines, professional journals, and newsletters that may be of interest to project managers. Information is provided on how to contact them, with no endorsement as to whether they are worthwhile.

La Cible. . . Le Journal du management de projet (published by AFITEP)

Association Francophone de Management de Projet
3, rue Francoise
75001 Paris, France
Tel: 42–36–36–37
FAX: 42–36–36–35

CrossTALK: The Journal of Defense Software Engineering

A free journal. You can reach them at www.STSC.Hill.AF.Mil/

Finnish Project Management Journal

Contact:

Editor-in-Chief, Associate Professor Karlos Artto
Helsinki University of Technology
P.O. Box 9500
02015 HUT, Finland
Tel: 358–9451–4751
FAX: 358–9451–3665
e-mail: Karlos.Artto@hut.fi

The International Journal of Project Management

Elsvier Science Ltd.
The Boulevard
Langford Lane Kidlington
Oxford OX5 1GB, England
Tel: 44(0)1865 843 010
e-mail: cdhelp@elsevier.co.uk

Project Management Journal

Project Management Institute Communications Office
323 West Main Street
Sylva, NC 28779
Tel: 704–586–3715
e-mail: pmnetwork@aol.com

PM NETWORK

Also published by Project Management Institute: see Project Management Journal.

ALLPM Today!

A free PM services vendor newsletter of ALL Project Management, an Internet Project Management resource center. See their web site: www.allpm.com

Business Process Strategies Newsletter

Download a free sample from the Cutter Information Corp.'s web site.

Project News

Balcombe Associates
Freepost (HR140)

Dilwyn, Herefordshire, England
Tel: 44(0)1544–388 848
FAX: 44(0)1544–388 400
e-mail: balcombe@pnews.kc3ltd.co.uk

Successful Project Management

Management Concepts
www.managementconcepts.com

Web Sites of Interest

Because the web is growing exponentially, this list will probably be out of date before the book is published, but perhaps it will get you started, and you will find links to other sites of interest. All web addresses begin with http://www.

pmforum.org
lewisinstitute.com
pmi.org
eiicorp.com

Other Resources

The following sources for information, books, and professional associations may be helpful in managing projects. Not all are specifically aimed at project management, but you may find them helpful, anyway.

Air Academy Press, L.L.C.

This group offers a very practical seminar on Design of Experiments. They also do training in Statistical Process Control. Their materials are first-class. Contact Steve Schmidt at 1155 Kelly Johnson Blvd., Suite 105, Colorado Springs, CO 80920. Tel: 719–531–0777. FAX: 719–531–0778.

CRM Films.

A good source of films for training, including *Mining Group Gold, The Abilene Paradox,* and many others. 2215 Faraday Ave., Carlsbad, CA 92008. Tel: 800–421–0833.

The Doug DeCarlo Group.

This is Doug DeCarlo's organization. Doug offers a variety of consulting and training programs. 88 Millstone Rd., Wilton, CT 06897. Tel: 203–762–7922. FAX: 203–762–2271. e-mail: idrum4pm@ix.optonline.net.

Enterprise Information Insights, Inc.

EII is a project management consulting organization that specializes in team formation, assessment, and development, as well as project office implementation and methodology development and integration. 4 Otsego Rd., Worcester, MA 01609. Tel: 508–791–2062. FAX: 508–791–2062. e-mail: rkw@eiicorp.com.

The Lewis Institute, Inc.

LII offers a certificate series in project management, together with courses for project team members. Other related courses are also available. 302 Chestnut Mountain Dr., Vinton, VA 24179. Tel: 540–345–7850. FAX: 540–345–7844. e-mail: jlewis@lewisinstitute.com.

MindWare.

The store for the other 90 percent of your brain. A source for tools, books, and other materials for helping enhance learning and creativity in organizations. They have a nice catalog listing their materials. 6142 Olson Memorial Hwy., Golden Valley, MN 55422. Tel: 800–999–0398. FAX: 612–595–8852.

Pegasus Communications.

Publishers of *The Systems Thinker,* a monthly newsletter. They also have videos by Russell Ackoff and Peter Senge, among others. P.O. Box 943, Oxford, OH 45056–0943. Tel: 800–636–3796. FAX: 905–764–7983.

Forms for Managing Projects

On our web site we have provided a number of forms for managing projects. These can be downloaded in PDF format, or in Word and WordPerfect format. Some spreadsheets are also available. Check www.lewisinstitute.com.

Project Manager
Skill Self-Assessment

On the following pages are self-assessment work sheets for you to use to assess your skills as a project manager. The complete skill profile of a project manager consists of fifty-four skills, as shown in Figure B.1.

To assess your proficiency level, use the Bloom's Taxonomy six-point scale introduced in Chapter Five and reproduced in Figure B.2.

Once you have completed the assessment, turn to Chapter Five and compare your profile with those of the four types of project managers shown in Figures 5.2 through 5.6. That should give you a good picture of the difference between your skill profile and those of each project manager type. This is called your "skill gap" and will be the basis of the tactical plans you will develop as part of your Career Development Plan (CDP).

Project Manager Skill Profile

Project Management Skills
Charter Development
Complexity Assessment
Cost Estimating
Cost Management
Critical Path Management
Detailed Estimating
Project Planning
Project Closeout
Project Management Software
Project Notebook Construction
Maintenance
Project Organization
Project Progress Assessment
Resource Acquisition
Resource Leveling
Resource Requirements
Schedule Development
Scope Management
Size Estimating

Management Skills
Delegation
Leadership
Managing Change
Managing Multiple Priorities
Meeting Management
Performance Management
Quality Management
Staff and Career Development
Staffing, Hiring, Selection

Business Skills
Budgeting
Business Assessment
Business Case Justification
Business Functions
Business Process Design
Company Products/Services
Core Applications System
Customer Service
Implementation
Planning: Strategic/Tactical
Product/Vendor Evaluation
Procedures and Policies
Systems Integration
Testing

Interpersonal Skills
Conflict Management
Flexibility
Influencing
Interpersonal Relations
Negotiating
Relationship Management
Team Management/Building

Personal Skills
Creativity
Decision Making/Critical Thinking
Presentations
Problem Solving/Trouble Shooting
Verbal Communications
Written Communications

FIGURE B-1   Project Manager Skill Profile

0: **unknown or n/a**
1: **Knowledge** (I can define it.)
2: **Comprehension** (I can explain how it works.)
3: **Application** (I have limited experience using it in simple situations.)
4: **Analysis** (I have extensive experience using it in complex situations.)
5: **Synthesis** (I can adapt it to other uses.)
6: **Evaluation** (I am recognized as an expert by my peers.)

FIGURE B-2   Bloom's Taxonomy

PROJECT MANAGEMENT SKILL SELF ASSESSMENT

Project Management Skills	Self-Assessed Skill Level						
	0	1	2	3	4	5	6
Charter Development							
Complexity Assessment							
Cost Estimating							
Cost Management							
Critical Path Management							
Detailed Estimating							
Project Planning (WBS, network, PERT, etc.)							
Project Closeout							
Project Management Software Expertise							
Project Notebook Construction & Maintenance							
Project Organization							
Project Progress Assessment							
Resource Acquisition							
Resource Levelling							
Resource Requirements							
Schedule Development							
Scope Management							
Size Estimating							
Personal Skills	0	1	2	3	4	5	6
Creativity							
Decision Making/Critical Thinking							
Presentations							
Problem Solving/Trouble Shooting							
Verbal Communications							
Written Communications							
Interpersonal Skills	0	1	2	3	4	5	6
Conflict Management							
Flexibility							
Influencing							
Interpersonal Relations							
Negotiating							
Relationship Management							
Team Management/Building							

FIGURE B-3a   Project Management Skill Self-Assessment

PROJECT MANAGEMENT SKILL SELF ASSESSMENT

Business Skills (continued)	0	1	2	3	4	5	6
Budgeting							
Business Assessment							
Business Case Justification							
Business Functions							
Business Process Design							
Company Products/Services							
Core Application Systems							
Customer Service							
Implementation							
Planning: Strategic and Tactical							
Product/Vendor Evaluation							
Standards, Procedures, Policies							
Systems and Technology Integration							
Testing							
Management Skills	0	1	2	3	4	5	6
Delegation							
Leadership							
Managing Change							
Managing Multiple Priorities							
Meeting Management							
Performance Management							
Quality Management							
Staff and Career Development							
Staffing, Hiring, Selection							

Self-Assessed Skill Level

FIGURE B-3b   Project Management Skill Self-Assessment (continued)

References and
Recommended Readings

Below is a list of books and articles related to career and professional development. They are grouped by major topic area to facilitate your finding titles that deal with specific topics of interest to you. Most of these titles are part of our personal library. We have found them useful and thought you might as well.

General Career

Anderson, Gary E., the First. *Shouldn't You Own Your Future Today? Linking Education to Skills In Quality Organizations.* Milwaukee: ASQC Quality Press, 1993. ISBN 0–87389–201–1.

Araoz, Daniel L., and William S. Sutton. *Reengineering Yourself: A Blueprint for Personal Success in the New Corporate Culture.* Holbrook, MA: Bob Adams Company, 1994. ISBN 1–55850–405–2.

Barkley, Nella, and Eric Sandburg. *Taking Charge of Your Career.* New York: Workman Publishing, 1995. ISBN 1–56305–495–7.

Bolles, Richard N. *What Color Is Your Parachute?* Berkeley, CA: Ten Speed Press, 2000. ISBN 1–58008–123–1.

Bridges, William. *Managing Transitions: Making the Most of Change.* Reading, MA: Addison-Wesley Publishing Company, 1991. ISBN 0–201–55073–3.

_____. *JobShift: How to Prosper in a Workplace Without Jobs.* Reading, MA: Addison-Wesley Publishing Company, 1994. ISBN 0–201–62667–5.

_____. *Creating You & Co.: Learn to think Like the CEO of Your Own Career*. Reading, MA: Addison-Wesley Publishing Company, 1997. ISBN 0–201–41987–4.

Deci, Edward L. *Why We Do What We Do: The Dynamics of Personal Autonomy*. New York: G. P. Putnam's Sons, 1995. ISBN 0–399–14047–6.

_____. *Why We Do What We Do: Understanding Self-Motivation*. New York: Penguin Books, 1995. ISBN 0–14–02–5526–5.

Farren, Caela. *Who's Running Your Career? Creating Stable Work In Unstable Times*. Austin, TX: Bard Press, 1997. ISBN 1–885167–17–2.

Hakim, Cliff. *We Are All Self-Employed*. San Francisco: Berrett-Koehler Publishers, 1994. ISBN 1–881052–47–8.

Hall, Douglas T., and Associates. *The Career Is Dead: Long Live the Career: A Relational Approach to Careers*. San Francisco: Jossey-Bass Publishers, 1996. ISBN 0–7879–0233–0.

Hansen, L. Sunny. *Integrative Life Planning: Critical Tasks for Career Development and Changing Life Patterns*. San Francisco: Jossey-Bass Publishers, 1997. ISBN 0–7879–0200–4.

Hummerow, Jean M. *New Directions in Career Planning and the Workplace*. Palo Alto: Consulting Psychologists Press, Inc., 1991. ISBN 0–89106–050–2.

Hyatt, Carole. *Lifetime Employability: How to Become Indispensable*. New York: Mastermedia Limited, 1995. ISBN 1–57101–027–0.

Johansen, Robert, and Rob Swigart. *Upsizing the Individual in the Downsized Organization*. Reading, MA: Addison-Wesley Publishers, 1994. ISBN 0–201–62712–4.

Kaye, Beverly L. *Up Is Not the Only Way: A Guide to Developing Workforce Talent*. Palo Alto: Davies-Black Publishing, 1997. ISBN 0–89106–099–5.

Kelly, Robert, and Janet Caplan. "How Bell Labs Creates Star Performers." *Harvard Business Review* (July-August 1993): 128–139.

Knox, Deborah L., and Sandra S. Butzel. *life work transitions.com*. Boston: Butterworth-Heinemann, 2000. ISBN 0–7506–7160–2.

Lareau, William. *The Where Am I Now? Where Am I Going? Career Manual*. Clinton, NJ: New Win Publishing, Inc., 1992. ISBN 0–8329–0464–3.

Leider, Richard J. *Life Skills: Taking Charge of Your Personal and Professional Growth*. San Diego: Pfeiffer & Company, 1994. ISBN 0–89384–230–3.

London, Manuel, ed. *Employees, Careers, and Job Creation*. San Francisco: Jossey-Bass Publishers, 1995. ISBN 0–7879–0125–3.

Marion, Peller. *Crisis Proof Your Career: Finding Job Security in an Insecure Time*. New York: Carol Publishing Group, 1993. ISBN 1–55972–181–2.

Moses, Barbara. *Career Intelligence: The 12 New Rules for Work and Life Success*. San Francisco: Berrett-Koehler Publishers, Inc., 1998. ISBN 1–57675–048–5.

Naisbett, John, and Patricia Aburdene. *Megatrends 2000*. New York: William Morrow and Company, 1990. ISBN 0–688–07224–0.

Peters, Tom. "The WOW Project." *Fast Company* (May 1999): 116–125.

Schein, Edgar H. *Career Anchors: Discovering Your Real Values*. San Diego: Pfeiffer & Company, 1990. ISBN 0–88390–030–0.

_____. *Career Survival: Strategic Job and Role Planning*. San Diego: Pfeiffer & Company, 1993. ISBN 0–88390–374–1.

Sher, Barbara. *Wishcraft: How to Get What You Really Want*. New York: Ballantine Books, 1979. ISBN 345–34089–2.

_____. *I Could Do Anything If I Only Knew What It Was*. New York: Dell Publishing, 1994. ISBN 0–440–50500–3.

Sims, Ronald R., and John G. Veres III, eds. *Keys to Employee Success in Coming Decades*. Westporet, CT: Quorum Books, 1999. ISBN 1–56720–194–6.

Tieger, Paul D., and Barbara Barron-Tieger. *Do What You Are: Discover the Perfect Career for You Through the Secrets of Personality Type*. Boston: Little, Brown and Company, 1995. ISBN 0–316–84522–1.

Whitten, Neal. *Becoming an Indispensable Employee in a Disposable World*. Englewood Cliffs, NJ: Prentice Hall, 1995. ISBN 0–13–603812–3.

Individual Skill Development

In this section we have further organized the references by skill area.

Conflict Management/Negotiating/Persuasion

Cialdini, Robert B. *The Power of Persuasion*. Rev. ed. New York: Quill, 1993. ISBN 0–68812–816–5.

Fisher, Roger, and William Ury. *Getting to Yes: Negotiating Agreement Without Giving In*. New York: Penguin Books, 1981. ISBN 0–14–00–6534–2.

Hamlin, Sonya. *How to Talk So People Listen*. New York: Harper & Row Publishers, 1988. ISBN 0–06–015669–4.

Kindler, Herbert S. *Managing Disagreement Constructively*. Los Altos, CA: Crisp Publications, Inc., 1988. ISBN 0–931961–41–6.

Creativity

Adams, James L. *Conceptual Blockbusting: A Guide to Better Ideas*. Reading, MA: Perseus Books, 1986. ISBN 0–201–55086–5.

De Bono, Edward. *Serious Creativity*. New York: HarperCollins, 1992.

Goman, Carol Kinsey. *Creativity in Business: A Practical Guide for Creative Thinking*. Los Altos, CA: Crisp Publications, Inc., 1989. ISBN 0–931961–67-X.

Hanks, Kurt, and Jay Parry. *Wake Up Your Creative Genius*. Los Altos, CA: Crisp Publications, Inc., 1991. ISBN 1–56052–111–2.

Herrmann, Ned. *The Creative Brain*. Lake Lure, NC: Brain Books, 1995. ISBN 0–944850–02–2.

_____. *The Whole Brain Business Book*. New York: McGraw-Hill, 1996.

Michalko, Michael. *Thinkertoys: A Handbook of Business Creativity*. Berkeley, CA: Ten Speed Press, 1991. ISBN 0898–154081.

Miller, William C. *Flash of Brilliance: Inspiring Creativity Where You Work*. Reading, MA: Perseus Books, 1999. ISBN 0–7382–0018–2.

_____. *The Flash of Brilliance Workbook*. Reading, MA: Perseus Books, 2000. ISBN 0–7382–0239–8.

Owens, James. *Innovation, Creativity and Handling Organizational Change*. Arlington, VA: Executive Publications, 1991.

Vance, Mike, and Dianne Deacon. *Think out of the Box*. Franklin Lakes, NJ: Career Press, 1995. ISBN 1–56414–186–1.

Von Oech, Roger. *A Whack on the Side of the Head*. New York: Warner Books, Inc., 1983. ISBN 0–446–38635–9.

_____. *A Kick in the Seat of the Pants*. New York: Harper & Rowe Publishers, 1986. ISBN 0–06–096024–8.

Leadership

Bennis, Warren. *On Becoming a Leader*. Reading, MA: Perseus Books, 1989. ISBN 0–201–40929–1.

Bennis, Warren, and Joan Goldsmith. *Learning to Lead*. Reading, MA: Perseus Books, 1997. ISBN 0–201–31140–2.

Brown, Carla L. *Techniques of Successful Delegation*. Shawnee Mission, KS: National Press Publications, Inc., 1988. ISBN 1–55852–015–5.

Champy, James, and Nitin Nohria. *The Arc of Ambition*. Reading, MA: Perseus Books, 2000. ISBN 0–7382–0103–0.

Jones, John E., and William L. Bearley. *360 Feedback: Strategies, Tactics, and Techniques for Developing Leaders*. Amherst, MA: HRD Press, 1996. ISBN 0–87425–356-X.

O'Neil, John. *Leadership Aikido.* New York: Harmony Books, 1997. ISBN 0–51770–575–3.

Owens, James. *Motivation at Work: The Key to Productivity.* Arlington, VA: Executive Publications, 1991.

Peterson, David B., and Mary Dee Hicks. *Leader As Coach: Strategies for Coaching and Developing Others.* Minneapolis, MN: Personnel Decisions International, 1996. ISBN 0–938529–14–5.

Pinto, Jeffrey K., and Jeffrey W. Trailer. *Leadership Skills for Project Managers.* Newton Square, PA: Project Management Institute, 1998. ISBN 1–880410–49–4.

Pinto, Jeffrey K. "Power and Politics: Managerial Implications." *PM Network* (August 1996): 36–39.

_____. *Power and Politics in Project Management.* Upper Darby, PA: Project Management Institute, 1996.

Tichy, Noel, and Eli Cohen. *The Leadership Engine: Building Leaders at Every Level.* Dallas, TX: Pritchett & Associates, Inc., 1998. ISBN 0–944002–25–0.

Personality

Keirsey, David, and Marilyn Bates. *Please Understand Me: Character and Temperament Types.* Del Mar, CA: Prometheus *Nemisis* Book Company, 1984. ISBN 0–9606954–0–0.

Keirsey, David. *Please Understand Me II.* Del Mar, CA: Prometheus *Nemisis* Book Company, 1998. ISBN 0–9606–954–7.

Kroeger, Otto, and Janet M. Thuesen. *Type Talk. Or How to Determine Your Personality Type and Change Your Life.* New York: Delacorte, 1988. ISBN 0–38529–828–5.

Marshall, Lisa J., and Lucy D. Freedman. *Smart Work: The Syntax Guide for Mutual Understanding in the Workplace.* Dubuque, IO: Kendall/ Hunt Publishing Company, 1995. ISBN 0-7872-0491-9.

Problem Solving and Decision Making

Arnold, John D. *The Complete Problem Solver: A Total System for Competitive Decision Making.* New York: John Wiley & Sons, Inc., 1993. ISBN 0-471-54198-2.

Chang, Richard Y., and P. Keith Kelly. *Step-By-Step Problem Solving.* Irvine, CA: Richard Chang Associates, Inc., 1993. ISBN 1-883553-11-3.

Couger, J. Daniel. *Creative Problem Solving and Opportunity Finding.* Danvers, MA: Boyd & Fraser Publishing Company, 1995. ISBN 0–87709–752–6.

Gause, Donald C., and Gerald M. Weinberg. *Are Your Lights On? How to Figure Out What the Problem Really Is.* New York: Dorset House Publishing, 1990. ISBN 0–932633–16–1.

Gelatt, H. B. *Creative Decision Making: Using Positive Uncertainty.* Los Altos, CA: Crisp Publications, Inc., 1991. ISBN 1–56052–098–1.

Owens, James. *Systems-type Decision Making and Management by Objectives.* Arlington, VA: Executive Publications, 1991.

Miscellaneous

Bloom, Benjamin S. *Taxonomy of Educational Objectives Book I: Cognitive Domain.* Longman, 1956.

Chang, Richard Y., and Kevin R. Kehoe. *Meetings That Work!* Irvine, CA: Richard Chang Associates, 1994. ISBN 1–883553–18–0.

Chopra, Deepak, M.D. *Magical Mind, Magical Body.* Audiotapes from Nightingale Conant, Niles Il, 1990.

Covey, Stephen R. *The 7 Habits of Highly Effective People.* New York: Simon & Schuster, 1989. ISBN 0–671–70863–5.

Dyer, Dr. Wayne. *You'll See It When You Believe It.* New York: Avon Books, 1989.

Elbeik, Sam, and Mark Thomas. *Project Skills.* Oxford, England: Butterworth-Heinemann, 1998. ISBN 0–7506–3978–4.

Frankl, Viktor E. *Man's Search for Meaning.* New York: Touchstone Books, 1984.

Gawain, Shakti. *The Path of Transformation.* Mill Valley, CA: Nataraj Publishing, 1993.

Jacobs, Ronald L., and Michael J. Jones. *Structured On-the-Job Training: Unleashing Employee Expertise in the Workplace.* San Francisco: Berrett-Koehler Publishers, 1995. ISBN 1–881052–20–6.

Klauser, Henriette Anne. *Writing on Both Sides of the Brain.* San Francisco: Harper Collins Publishers, 1986. ISBN 0–06–254490-X.

Macdonald, John. *Calling a Halt to Mindless Change.* New York: Amacom, 1998.

Peck, M. Scott, M.D. *The Road Less Traveled.* New York: Touchstone Books, 1978.

Spencer, Lyle M., and Signe M. Spencer. *Competence at Work: Models for Superior Performance.* New York: John Wiley & Sons, Inc., 1993. ISBN 0–471–54809-X.

Verma, Vijay K. *Human Resource Skills for the Project Manager*. Newton Square, PA: Project Management Institute, 1996. ISBN 1 880410–41–9.

Team Effectiveness

Belbin, R. Meredith. *Management Teams: Why They Succeed Or Fail*. Oxford, England: Butterworrth-Heinemann, 1981. ISBN 0–7506–0253–8.

_____. *Team Roles at Work*. Oxford, England: Butterworth-Heinemann, 1993. ISBN 0–7506–2675–5.

_____. *Changing the Way We Work*. Oxford, England: Butterworth-Heinemann, 1997. ISBN 0–7506–4288–2.

Duarte, Deborah L., and Nancy Tennant Snyder. *Mastering Virtual Teams*. San Francisco: Jossey-Bass Publishers, 1999. ISBN 0–7879–4183–2.

Eales-White, Rupert. *How to Be a Better Teambuilder*. London: Kogan Page Ltd., 1996. ISBN 0–7494–1912–1.

Harris, Jean. *Sharpen Your Team's Skills in Project Management*. London: The McGraw-Hill Companies, 1997. ISBN 0–07–709140-X.

Hayward, Martha. *Managing Virtual Teams: Practical Techniques for High-Technology Project Managers*. Boston: Artech House, 1998. ISBN 0–89006–913–1.

Huszczo, Gregory E. *Tools for Team Excellence*. Palo Alto, CA: Davies-Black Publishing, 1996. ISBN 0–89106–081–2.

Isgar, Thomas. *The Ten Minute Team*. Boulder: Seluera Press, 1993. ISBN 0–9623464–1–1.

Jones, Peter H. *Handbook of Team Design*. New York: McGraw-Hill, 1998. ISBN 0–07–032880–3.

Katzenbach, Jon R., and Douglas K. Smith. *The Wisdom of Teams: Creating the High-Performance Organization*. Boston: Harvard Business School Press, 1993. ISBN 0–87584–367–0.

Lewis, James. *Team-Based Project Management*. New York: Amacom, 1997. ISBN 0–8144–0364–6.

Lipman-Blumen, Jean, and Harold J. Leavitt. *Hot Groups: Seeding Them, Feeding Them and Using Them to Ignite Your Organization*. New York: Oxford University Press, 1999. ISBN 0–19–512686–6.

Margerison, Charles, and Dick McCann. *Team Management: Practical New Approaches*. Glucestershire, England: Management Books 2000 Ltd., 1995. ISBN 1–85252–114–7.

_____. *Team Reengineering: Using the Language of Teamwork*. Brisbane, Australia: Team Management Systems, 1995. ISBN 0–646–22362–3.

Moxon, Peter. *Building a Better Team*. Hampshire, England: Gower Publishing, 1993. ISBN 0–566–08007–9.

Smith, Steve. *Build That Team!* London: Kogan Page Ltd., 1997. ISBN 0–7494–2483–4.

Sundstrom, Eric, and Associates. *Supporting Work Team Effectiveness*. San Francisco: Jossey-Bass Publishers, 1999. ISBN 0–7879–4322–3.

Syer, John, and Christopher Connolly. *How Teamwork Works: The Dynamics of Effective Team Development*. London: The McGraw-Hill Companies, 1996. ISBN 0–07–707942–6.

Thompson, Leigh. *Making the Team*. Upper Saddle River, NJ: Prentice Hall, 2000. ISBN 0–13–014363–4.

Verma, Vijay K. *Managing the Project Team*. Upper Darby, PA: Project Management Institute, 1997. ISBN 1–880410–42–7.

Miscellaneous

Goldratt, Eliyahu M. *Critical Chain: A Business Novel*. Great Barrington, MA: North River Press, 1997. ISBN 0–88427–153–6.

Graham, Robert J., and Randall L. Englund. *Creating an Environment for Successful Projects*. San Francisco: Jossey-Bass Publishers, 1997. ISBN 0–7879–0359–0.

Kerzner, Harold. *In Search of Excellence in Project Management*. New York: Van Nostrand Reinhold, 1998. ISBN 0–442–02706–0.

Lewis, James. *Project Planning, Scheduling and Control*. Rev. ed. Chicago: Irwin Professional Publishing, 1995. ISBN 1–55738–869–5.

_____. *Mastering Project Management*. New York: McGraw-Hill, 1998. ISBN 0–7863–1188–6.

_____. *The Project Manager's Desk Reference*. 2nd ed. New York: McGraw-Hill, 2000. ISBN 0–07–134750–X.

Project Management Institute. *A Guide to the Project Management Body of Knowledge*. Upper Darby, PA: The Project Management Institute, 1996. ISBN 1–880410–13–3.

Wysocki, Robert K., et al. *Effective Project Management*. 2nd ed. New York: John Wiley & Sons, Inc., 2000. ISBN 0–471–36028–7.